Dump It & Forget It Paleo 5 Minute Paleo Slow Cooker Recipes for Delicious and Simple Paleo Meals

By: Natalie Jane

Table of Contents

Introduction

The paleo movement is catching fire! You have probably read up on what the plan is, you have heard the success stories of how the plan has completely changed people's lives, maybe you have even dabbled with some paleo friendly recipes, but like many, you have probably found yourself overwhelmed at the prospect of having to do so much work in the kitchen. Between the food prep, the cooking, and the cleanup afterward, many people can be put off by the prospect of changing their lives. Luckily, a handy little gadget in your kitchen can facilitate your transition into a new lifestyle without breaking a sweat!

With the help of your crockpot, you can transform almost any dish into a healthy, paleo-friendly, one that requires no more than a couple of minutes of your time. Just dump a couple of ingredients into your slow cooker before leaving in the morning, and come home to the wonderful aroma of a home cooked meal that is delicious *and* healthy! Each of the recipes included in this book requires only five ingredients, but each one is jam packed with nutrients that are lacking in the typical American diet. Never before has it been so easy to transition into a new eating lifestyle!

Enclosed, you will find some dishes that you could find in your favorite restaurants like sausage and peppers, whole roast chicken, and BBQ ribs alongside some international ones to broaden your horizon and expand your flavor profile, but the beautiful thing is that each only requires a handful of ingredients and a couple of moments from your busy schedule to throw them in your slow cooker. You don't need to be a trained chef or even have any experience at all to create these culinary masterpieces in your own kitchen.

No more excuses! You know that the paleo movement is real and can make a lasting impact in your life. What are you waiting for? Take a look through the recipes included here, try some out, and change your life once and for all. You will surely be amazed by how easy they are to create, how amazing they taste, and just how much this change in your lifestyle can positively impact the health, wellness, and happiness of you and your family!

Chapter 1: What Does It Mean To Eat Paleo?

Beginning a paleo diet means only consuming food that would have been available to an average human being during the Paleolithic period, a timeframe during human development that runs from 2.6 million years ago to about 10,000 years ago. Even though there is some speculation about what exactly the menu looked like back then, there is a general consensus about what varieties of food would have been available for hunter/gatherer humans.

A quick list of 'staple' paleo foods would include:

- Meat (chicken, beef, turkey and other fowl)

- Fish

- Fruit

- Eggs

- Vegetables

- Nuts and seeds

- Oils derived from healthy, natural sources (olives, avocados, coconuts, etc.)

This may seem a little too bland for your tastes. But don't fret, because included in this book are recipes that combine the above ingredients with acceptable seasonings to make for truly delicious meals that you will actually look forward to eating. That being said, there are many, many modern foods which need to be avoided in order to maintain compliance with a paleo diet. Some of those foods are:

- Refined sugars

- Processed food

- Candy

- Dairy

- Potatoes and potato-based foods

- Foods high in sodium content

This list rules out most dessert plates as well as anything with cheese, cream or heavy salt. You might think this is easy to do, but after a few days on a paleo diet, you will begin to feel your body missing these creature comfort foods. Thankfully, foods high in fiber can help with these cravings by taking your mind off of food for a while so that you can focus on something else.

Remember that just about any kind of meat is considered paleo-friendly with the exception being highly processed meats like hot dogs, bratwurst, and Spam. This means that you can indulge in meat that you may not otherwise eat regularly.

Chapter 2: Myths and Misconceptions

You have undoubtedly heard rumors and misinformation about many various 'fad' diets – some of them do hold water, but most of them are greatly exaggerated and do not comport with reality. Because every human body needs food to function and because every single one of us has to fuel our bodies in some way, there are as many anecdotal half-truths about dieting as there are scientifically-backed facts. The challenge becomes weeding through the 'noise' to get to what is actually true and effective.

In this chapter, we will highlight these myths, mentally preparing you for what to expect as you forge forward on your journey of switching to a Paleo diet.

Some of the diets you've probably come across may include:

- The Atkins Diet

- The Keto (or 'Ketogenic') Diet

- Liquid Fasting Diets

- Toxin Cleansing Diets

- Low Carb Diets

...the list goes on.

Each of these diets has a general theme that accompanies it. For example: in the case of the Atkins Diet, the theme is to eat low-carb foods that are counterbalanced with foods high in fiber and saturated fats. The most common myth associated with the Atkins diet is that you won't have any energy to do anything because your body will be constantly depleted of glycogen, a source of energy derived from carbohydrates (among other sources).

As you might have guessed, this is simply untrue. The human body has an amazing way of adapting to the nutritional environment it is placed in, and our metabolism will adjust itself accordingly. This often means that after a few weeks of eating nothing but low-carb, high-fat and high-protein foods, our bodies react by metabolizing fat faster and by not relying heavily on carbohydrates as an energy source.

So what about Paleo?

The biggest misconception about the paleo diet has to do with assumptions that are made about what exactly our ancient human ancestors ate on a regular basis. There seems to be a lot of confusion about what humans in the Paleolithic era (the era after which the paleo diet got its name) consumed, but a little research reveals some key facts that are worth remembering:

Myth: Our ancestors did not eat beans (legumes) or whole grains.

This is flatly false. Dating back to 30,000 years ago, stone-grinding implements used for breaking down seeds and grains into a flour-like compound have been found in Europe and parts of the central Mediterranean. An example of such a tool is the mortar and pestle, known for being used to finely crush dry material into a kind of powder that can be used in rudimentary baking.

Further, archaeologists have determined that human beings who lived in the Paleolithic era did, in fact, consume legumes and grains, judging from an analysis of their fossilized tooth plaque.

Myth: We can eat exactly what Paleolithic Man ate, with modern foods.

Even though it's a nice thought, this simply cannot be done. Why?

The reason is because food today is the product of guided mutations, cross-breeding, and genetic modification, all of which renders it completely foreign when compared with the diet of a human being who lived 10,000 years in the past. Even going to the supermarket to buy a few pieces of lean meat like chicken or fish requires that you select from meat that was raised in a way that would be unthinkable 10 millennia ago.

Myth: Restricted diets like paleo are expensive because they require you to eat special foods.

The beauty of shopping for food while on the paleo diet is that most of what you need are simple, available and often cheap if you buy in bulk. Meat can be purchased in large quantities, and most unused portions can be frozen. The same can be said for most of the vegetables that many paleo recipes call for. Moreover, with effective meal planning techniques like those covered in this book, costs per meal can realistically reach the sub-$5.00 range. Obviously, this depends on your nutritional requirements.

Even though there are more, these are some of the most commonly spread myths surrounding the paleo diet. We'll now get into more of a technical look at the diet itself, and we'll start breaking down the ingredients for each meal in a typical, 7-day week.

Chapter 3: Days 1-5

Healthy Pad Thai

We are all familiar with this delicious Thai dish. However, the traditional recipe is full of sugar and paired with carbohydrate rich noodles. To enjoy a healthy and delicious meal with all the flavors of the traditional dish, enjoy our recipe below.

INGREDIENTS

1 cup of Coconut Milk

1 Cup of Chicken Stock

2 Full TBSP of Sunflower Seed Butter (this is in place of the peanut flavor; you can also use freshly pressed peanut butter)

1 TBSP of Soy Sauce and/or Fish Sauce

Add Garlic Cloves and Ginger to attain the spice you desire.

Pair this Sauce with:

2-3lbs of Chicken Thighs or Breasts (make sure to remove the skin prior to using), or any kind of meat or vegetables you choose.

Optional:

You can also add green onions, cashews, cilantro, or red pepper flakes depending on your flavor preferences.

DIRECTIONS

Add the coconut milk, chicken stock, peanut/sunflower butter, soy sauce, fish sauce, garlic and ginger, and any other additional optional ingredients. Place the meat of your choice into the base liquid. You can also add vegetables to the top of the crock pot, making sure not to place in the liquid. You only want to steam the vegetables, not stew them. Depending on the size of your crock pot, cook your meal for 4 hours if you are using a 4-quart crock pot, and 5-6 hours if you are using a 6-quart crock pot. Remove from crock pot and enjoy with zucchini noodles or butternut squash noodles!

Slow Cooker Pull-Apart Beef

If you are looking for an easy and spicy option for dinner with very little time, this recipe is going to be a big hit. With the flavors of the Southwest mixed with the spice of the chilies, you will enjoy making this recipe over and over!

INGREDIENTS

2 lbs. of Beef Chuck Roast

1 TBSP of your favorite Southwestern spice blend

2-3 tsp. of Olive Oil

8 oz. of Diced Green Chiles including the juice

DIRECTIONS

Take the beef and make sure to trim all the undesirable parts of the chuck roast off. Once you are done with that, cut the chuck roast into thin strips. When you trim the beef, you will find that your beef will reduce in size, so if you purchase a 3 lb. beef chuck roast, then you will most likely end up with 2 lbs. of beef. Make sure the strips are small even after trimming the beef.

Take each strip of beef and rub it down with the seasoning mixture, then you want to add your oil, between 2-3 TBSP (depending on your pan), and add the beef strips. Make sure to brown the outside of the beef strips on all sides, this browning process adds flavor and caramelizes the outside of the beef.

Place the strips of the browned beef into your slow cooker and add the diced green chilies and the juice, on top. Turn your crock pot to the 3-4 hour option. If you are going to be out for a while, you can also set the crock pot to low, and cook for 6-8 hours. The beef should pull apart easily at this point. You want to use a slotted spoon to remove the beef from the crock pot and set on a cutting board. Using two forks, shred the beef apart and then place back in the slow cooker so the beef can absorb the additional liquid.

You can enjoy this beef by itself, over vegetables, beans, or cauliflower rice. Enjoy!

Roasted Pork and Apples

What goes better with pork than apples? This paleo pork will melt in your mouth, and the protein and fiber from the apples will leave you feeling full all day. Nothing will come close to welcoming you home like the smell of this wonderful dish when you get home from a long day at work.

INGREDIENTS

3-5 pound pork roast (shoulder or butt work best)

7 apples (gala and pink delicious seem to work best)

¼ cup apple cider vinegar

1 TSP ground ginger

¼ cup brown sugar

Optional:

Feel free to add some cinnamon as it really goes well with the brown sugar and apples.

DIRECTIONS

In a large pan, brown the pork using high heat. While the pork browns, chop apples into the desired size (sliced or chopped), and layer them down at the bottom of the slow cooker. Once the pork is browned, lay it on top of the apples. In a small bowl, mix the vinegar, ginger, and brown sugar. Then pour over the top of the roast. Sweet potatoes go perfectly with this dish!

Pumpkin Pie Oatmeal

Nothing will pull you out of bed in the morning like waking up to the smell of this oatmeal! Great for warming up your soul on those cold mornings, this oatmeal has the added benefit of pumpkin for additional vitamin A and fiber.

INGREDIENTS

2 cups of steel cut oats

1 can of pureed pumpkin

2 cups coconut milk

2 TSP cinnamon

1 TSP brown sugar

DIRECTIONS

Mix together the oats, pureed pumpkin, coconut milk, cinnamon, and brown sugar until evenly distributed, and cook on low for three hours. Your slow cooker will keep it nice and warm for when you wake up in the morning. There are tons of great options for toppings from toasted almonds, pumpkin seeds, raisins, or pecans. Experiment and enjoy.

Maple Syrup Chicken

Getting bored with savory? This sweet maple chicken will snap your savory streak and have you begging for seconds. This dish works great on it's own or kicked up to a whole other level with some added heat.

INGREDIENTS

4 Chicken breasts or thighs, skinless

1 large yellow onion, chopped

3 TBSP real maple syrup

5 sprigs of thyme, fresh

2 sweet potatoes

Optional:

Kick up the heat with some chili powder, cayenne, or red chili pepper flakes.

DIRECTIONS

Remove any skin from the breasts and sear in hot pan. Lightly mix the maple syrup and optional spice and coat the chicken. Add ingredients to the crockpot, leaving the sweet potatoes whole.

Chapter 4: Days 6-10

Salsa Verde Chicken

While this may be the simplest of recipes with only three ingredients, don't be tricked into thinking that it will be lacking in flavor. This zesty Mexican dish will provide you with the protein your body needs and the flavor your tongue craves.

INGREDIENTS

3 pounds of boneless skinless chicken breasts

1 TBSP ghee

1 16 ounce jar of salsa verde

DIRECTIONS

Coat the bottom of a large pan with the ghee over high heat. Gently brown the breasts before adding them to the slow cooker with the salsa verde. You can either shred the chicken half of the way through the cooking, or you can leave it whole and brown them a second time. This will add a nice texture to the outside while still being moist and delicious on the inside.

Chicken Satay

Enjoy all the flavor that Indian dishes bring without any of the slaving away at the stove. This is a great dish to bring some international flair to your cooking repertoire and some great flavor profile to your chicken. Great for entertaining guests or enjoy all the leftovers for days to come.

INGREDIENTS

4 boneless skinless chicken breasts

1 12 ounce can of coconut milk

4 cloves of crushed garlic

1 TBSP fresh ground ginger

1 TBSP curry paste

DIRECTIONS

Brown the chicken breasts in a pan over high heat. While the chicken browns, add the crushed garlic, ground ginger, and curry paste into the slow cooker with the coconut milk. Mix until ingredients are evenly distributed and add the chicken. For a richer, creamier option, you can use coconut cream instead of the coconut milk. This dish goes great with sweet potatoes!

Whole Chicken in a Pot

Whether you are entertaining guests or just want to make sure that you have already prepared protein ready for the week, this whole chicken will give you plenty of options with a minimal amount of work, and the aromatics will have this tender chicken bursting with flavor.

INGREDIENTS

1 whole roasting chicken

2 sprigs of rosemary

4 sprigs of thyme

4 cloves of garlic

1 onion, quartered

DIRECTIONS

Remove plastic ties and innards from the chicken and discard (unless you want to make a gravy later). Place the bird breast side down in the pot and distribute the garlic, onion, rosemary, and thyme around it. This bird should be falling off the bone at the 6-7 hour mark! Feel free to add some carrots or tubers in there if you have the room. Feel free to hang onto the carcass for the next recipe!

Coconut Curry Beef

Take a trip to India with this flavorful and tasty curry recipe. Curry typically has copious amounts of additional sugar and unhealthy ingredients when you order at your local Indian restaurant. Now, you can achieve the same flavors without the unnecessary additives!

INGREDIENTS

2 lbs. of Beef Stew Meat, you can find this at your local grocery store, it will be trimmed in 1-inch cubes

1 14oz can of coconut milk

2 rounded TBSP of Curry Powder

Vegetables of your choosing: Traditional 1 onion, 3-4 carrots, 1 head cauliflower and 1 cup celery are added and provide the best flavor profile

(Optional: 1/2-1 teaspoon of salt can be added at the very end. Add to your taste.)

DIRECTIONS

To begin, add the coconut milk and curry powder to the crock pot. Make sure to stir so the curry powder is well incorporated. Then add your stew meat and mix all the ingredients together. Next, add your vegetables of your choosing and mix well. Set your crock pot to cook on low for 8-10 hours. Serve over quinoa, brown rice, or enjoy by itself!

Chicken Vegetable Broth

This is a perfect follow up the recipe to the previous one. Rather than discarding the leftover remnants of the chicken, utilize the bones for a savory broth as the base for a vegetable soup. This is a perfect dish to warm your soul on a cold day or nurse you back to health when you aren't feeling well, and it freezes nicely to save for a rainy day!

INGREDIENTS

1 Leftover roasting chicken carcass

7 carrots, chopped

5 stalks of celery, chopped

1 large yellow onion, chopped

2 bay leaves

DIRECTIONS

Add all your ingredients to the slow cooker and fill with water. Cook on high for 12 hours or longer. Use a colander with small holes or even a cheesecloth to strain out any bits of bone and pour broth through into a large bowl. This works great when done overnight as you can add the broth to a thermos to take on the go to work.

Chapter 5: Days 11-15

Hawaiian Pork

Nothing says Hawaii like pulled pork! This recipe is a quick and easy take on slow-cooked pork that isn't that far off from the traditional pig roasts of the islands. Feel free to go larger on the cut of meat as the leftovers are to die for!

INGREDIENTS

Large Pork Butt (3-5 lbs)

1-2 TSP course sea salt

4 slices of uncured bacon

5 cloves of garlic

1 yellow onion, chopped

DIRECTIONS

Lie out the slices of bacon across the bottom of the pot and coat the pork with about ½ a TSP per pound of meat. Add in the peeled garlic and chopped onion. After 8-10 hours, shred pork with a couple of forks.

By now you should hear the waves crashing against the shore and find your belly wanting to dance with joy! The leftovers make for perfect tacos, too!

Red Wine Beef Roast

Red wine just has a way of making any beef dish just a little bit better. Many forget that you can add it as an ingredient to slow cooker recipes, and this one really does the trick. Just make sure that you don't skimp on the quality of the wine; if it is good enough to drink, it is good enough to cook with.

INGREDIENTS

3 pounds of beef pot roast

1 cup of red wine (varietal not important)

2 cloves of garlic

2 TSP cracked pepper

2 TSP salt

DIRECTIONS

Brown beef roast in a large pan over high heat. Add into the slow cooker on low for about ten hours. If you have room, feel free to add in some carrots and/or potatoes.

Pork and Cabbage Stew

Cabbage is an often-overlooked vegetable that is actually loaded with phytochemicals and micronutrients. This pork and cabbage stew may not be your momma's stew, but it would have been if she had this recipe!

INGREDIENTS

2-3 pounds pork butt

1 small head of cabbage (doesn't matter the color), shredded

2 bell peppers, chopped

1 onion, chopped

3 cups of chopped carrots

DIRECTIONS

Brown your pork roast in a large pan over high heat. While that sears, chop up your vegetables and place in a large bowl. Once the meat has browned, place it in the slow cooker, and evenly distribute the vegetables on top. Add salt and pepper to taste and add 2 cups of liquid (vegetable/beef broth or water). Let it cook for at least 10 hours to get fully tender.

Southwest Chicken

Here is an awesome, easy recipe that allows you a great deal of flexibility in how much of a kick it gives; just pick the appropriate salsa! This south of the border chicken dish will have you saying, "Mas pollo, por favor!"

INGREDIENTS

4 boneless skinless chicken breasts

1 bag of frozen corn

1 ½ cups of chopped bell pepper

2 cups of chunky salsa (pick one with the desired amount of spice)

1 large yellow onion, chopped

DIRECTIONS

Brown the chicken breasts in a large pan over high heat. Lay the chopped bell pepper, corn, and yellow onion on the bottom of the cooker. Add the chicken breasts once browned, and pour the salsa over the top. Buenvenido to flavor!

Irish Beef Stew

Slow cookers were made for stew. This one is simple yet delicious. The meat falls apart with each bite, and you will soon find your bowl empty and your belly full! Feel free to add in some additional goodies if the mood strikes you.

INGREDIENTS

3 pounds beef stew meat

2 cups green peas

3 bay leaves

2 cups chopped potatoes

2 cups chopped carrots

DIRECTIONS

Brown stew meat in a large pan over high heat. Add peas, bay leaves, potatoes, carrots, and meat to the slow cooker then add water or beef broth to cover ingredients. Set it for low and slow and watch your mouth water in anticipation. Stir in some coconut flour to thicken to desired consistency if needed.

Chapter 6: Days 16-20

Sausage and Kale Soup

Ah, kale, everyone's favorite vegetable these days and with good reason. This superfood is one of the most nutrient-dense plants on the planet. The sausage in the soup adds a warm savory goodness that your soul craves, while the kale is the paleo equivalent of taking your daily vitamin. This is a dish that really does an amazing job of balancing taste with nutrition.

INGREDIENTS

2 pounds of ground sausage

2 cups chopped kale

1 onion, chopped

2 cloves of garlic, crushed

2 cups of carrots, chopped

DIRECTIONS

Cover the bottom of the slow cooker with the ground sausage. Add in the kale-onion, garlic, and carrots; then pour in two cups of liquid (broth, stock, or water). Let the slow cooker do its thing on low heat for 8-10 hours and enjoy a hearty filling soup.

BBQ Chicken Apple Stew

This recipe seemed a bit odd at first, but the mixture of flavors and textures really play well together. This dish is a great one to impress your adventurous friends, as they have likely never thought of doing anything like this before! Demonstrate your mastery over the slow cooker and revel in the oohs and awes around the table.

INGREDIENTS

2 pounds of boneless skinless chicken thighs

2 apples, diced

2 onions diced

1 head of cauliflower

1 jar of your favorite BBQ sauce (12 ounces)

DIRECTIONS

Dice up your apples and onions to the same size. Take your cauliflower and grate it down to cauliflower rice (your food processor can do this quickly if you have one on hand). Add the cauliflower rice, apples, onion, and BBQ sauce into the pot and mix until evenly distributed. Add in the raw chicken thighs, making sure that they are fully submerged in the mixture, cover, and cook for 8-10 hours. Your friends and neighbors will magically show up at your door once the amazing smell reaches them.

Pepper Encrusted Pot Roast

Who says you even need five ingredients for an amazing, nutritious meal? This dish really gets to the heart of paleo in its simplicity. A good quality beef and rosemary will take you far in the culinary world!

INGREDIENTS

2-3 lbs. of a cut of beef of your choosing. Beef Chuck Roast typically is inexpensive and works well with crock pot recipes.

Salt and Pepper to taste

1 Sprig of Fresh Rosemary

INSTRUCTIONS

With a paper towel, pat the beef down and then rub with salt and fresh cracked pepper on all sides of the meat. Make sure to press the seasoning firmly into the meat. Add Olive Oil to a pan and sear all sides of the meat, making sure to get a deep golden brown, but not burn, on the meat. Searing not only caramelizes the meat, but it also locks in all the juices contained within the meat.

Add the chuck roast, or whatever cut of meat you chose, to the crock pot along with the sprig of rosemary. Set your crock pot to the low setting and cook for 8 hours. You can also set the crock pot to high and cook your meat for 6 hours instead.

You now have a delicious and tender main dish prepared. This recipe is great for leftovers too, on tacos, in casseroles, and with vegetables.

Chocolate Almond Butter Oatmeal

I tend to eat this dish as often for dessert as I do for breakfast. It is extremely filling, but more importantly, it tastes like heaven. If a peanut butter cup and almond butter oatmeal had a baby, this would be it. I will leave it up to you whether you set this up before bed to have as breakfast or before you leave for work as a treat to entice you back home. Either way, you are in for a treat.

INGREDIENTS

2 cups steel cut oats

2 cups coconut milk

1 TBSP almond butter

1 TBSP unsweetened cocoa powder

1 TBSP brown sugar

DIRECTIONS

In a small blender, blend the coconut milk and cocoa powder until evenly mixed. (The cocoa powder is usually too stubborn to mix with a spoon). Combine all the ingredients in the slow cooker, mixing until an even consistency. Cook on low for three hours, and enjoy. Don't worry if you don't get back to it at exactly three hours. Your slow cooker will keep it perfectly warm and scrumptious until you get around to waking up or getting home.

Butternut Squash Chicken Soup

Butternut squash isn't necessarily something that you think of when you are pondering what to throw in the crock-pot, but it is a great addition to many paleo friendly slow cooker dishes. This soup has an amazing balance of sweet and savory that will delight the pallet and break up the monotony of your work week.

INGREDIENTS

2-3 pounds of boneless skinless chicken (thighs or breasts), chopped into cubes

2 TBSP coconut oil

2 pounds of butternut squash, cubed

1 onion, diced

10 figs (make sure you remove all the stems), chopped small

Optional:

You can zest up the chicken with the addition of some rosemary, garlic, salt, and pepper.

DIRECTIONS

Add the coconut oil to a hot pan and brown your chicken over high heat. Add the onions in to caramelize them. Once the onions and chicken are browned, add them to the slow cooker with the butternut squash and figs. If you want more of a soup consistency, add in a cup of water or chicken stock. You can skip this step if you prefer a thicker, stew-like, consistency.

Put your slow cooker on low for 6-8 hours, and come home to a wonderful, novel soup!

Chapter 7: Days 21-25

Thai Beef

This Thai beef recipe leaves the stew meat so tender and delicious that it has completely changed the way I view Asian stews. There are a ton of options to play with in the vegetable additions. Each one adds a subtle flavor that can really change up the dish.

INGREDIENTS

3 pounds of stew meat

1 can of coconut milk

2 TBSP of curry powder or paste

1 chopped onion

1 cup celery

Optional:
Carrots, parsnip, cauliflower, and green peas all work as great vegetable additions

DIRECTIONS:
In a large pan over high heat, brown the stew meat. You will probably need to brown it in several batches to get a good sear on the meat. While the meat browns, add chopped onion, celery, curry, and coconut milk, mixing until evenly distributed. Add stew meat, set it, and forget it until a wonderful aroma fills your house.

Sausage and Peppers

Peppers are jam packed with vitamin C and other important nutrients to keep your body going, and the combination of fat, protein and fiber is enough to keep you full for hours. This is also another example of a crock-pot version of a traditional dish that is infinitely easier to prepare with the same results.

INGREDIENTS

2 pounds ground sausage

2 onions, chopped

2 apples, chopped

6 bell peppers, chopped

3 cloves of garlic, crushed

DIRECTIONS

Add the meat to the bottom of your slow cooker and pile on the apples, onions, peppers, and garlic. Cook on low for 8-10 hours. When it is done, give it a good stir that breaks up the sausage at the bottom into more manageable chunks. Enjoy!

Creamy Butternut Squash Soup

One thing that many people seem to not realize is that you can easily get a pureed soup with the help of your trusty slow cooker. This smooth and creamy butternut squash soup is absolutely amazing! Whether it is a lead into a larger meal or a stand-alone meal, it will surely leave you satisfied and smiling.

INGREDIENTS

2 pounds of chopped butternut squash

2 cups of chopped carrots

1 onion, chopped

½ TBSP ginger

½ TBSP cinnamon

DIRECTIONS

Add all the ingredients to the slow cooker and cook on low for 6-8 hours. By this point, the vegetables should be nice and tender. Remove the ingredients and put them in your blender or food processor with some liquid (adding coconut cream is an awesome addition) and puree until nice and smooth in consistency. Garnish with a sprig of mint and dazzle your houseguests with something you just whipped up in minutes.

Pumpkin Chicken Stew

I always keep a couple extra cans of pumpkin puree in my pantry to be able to whip up this delicious chicken dish. The combination of the sweet pumpkin and the juicy, tender chicken just seems to always end my day with a smile. Not only that, this stew is brimming with vitamin A, fiber, and other important nutrients.

INGREDIENTS

2 pounds of boneless skinless chicken (thighs or breasts), cubed

3 cans of pumpkin puree

2 onions, diced

2 cups of carrots, chopped

1 can of coconut milk

DIRECTIONS

No need to brown the chicken since it is in small cubes. Instead, just mix the coconut milk and pumpkin puree inside the slow cooker. Add in the onion, carrots, and chicken, making sure that everything is evenly distributed. After 8-10 hours, you should have a very unique, delicious, and nutritious stew!

BBQ Beef Ribs

I usually am not a huge fan of beef ribs as they tend to be far tougher than pork ones. The slow cooker solves this problem by ensuring that they literally fall off of the bone while still giving you that robust beef flavor that pork ribs don't have. This recipe will surely make you a lover of beef ribs as well!

INGREDIENTS

3 pounds of beef ribs

2 sprigs of rosemary

1 bottle of your favorite BBQ sauce

DIRECTIONS

Add the ribs and rosemary into your slow cooker with salt and pepper to taste, but hold off on adding the BBQ sauce. Cook the ribs on low for 10-12 hours. Once they are done, place the ribs in an oven safe dish and baste them with the BBQ sauce. Pop the dish in the oven at 400 degrees for ten minutes before serving. This will give a nice texture to the ribs and a layered flavor profile that you wouldn't get otherwise.

Chapter 8: Days 26-30

Beef Cabbage Stew

This is a stew that is as hearty on flavor as it is in nutrients. Instead of a traditional stew, this one is supercharged with cabbage, rutabaga, and onion. Just because it is five ingredients, doesn't mean it doesn't pack a nutritional punch!

INGREDIENTS

2 pounds of stew meat

2 onions, chopped

2 pounds of rutabaga, chopped

1 head of cabbage (color not important), sliced

2 TBSP of fish sauce

DIRECTIONS

Brown your stew meat in a pan over high heat, searing in the juices. Once browned, use the pan to caramelize the onions over medium heat with some olive oil to prevent sticking. In the slow cooker, add a cup of liquid (broth or water) and fish sauce. Stir until well mixed and add the rest of the ingredients. Cook for 8-10 hours on low. Add in coconut flour while mixing to thicken stew to desired consistency.

Arroz Con Pollo

This Costa Rican staple is amazing! This paleo friendly dish has a great ratio of carbs, fats, and proteins, but more importantly, it tastes like heaven. I can't seem to get enough, and with it being so easy to throw together, you can have it whenever you want!

INGREDIENTS

4 boneless skinless chicken breasts

2 cups white rice

1 TSP cumin

1 cup green peas

1 can plum tomatoes

Optional:

Cilantro, garlic, and bell peppers, and really give this dish a whole new level of awesome flavor.

DIRECTIONS

Brown the chicken breasts in a pan over high heat. Mix the rice, cumin, peas, tomatoes, and liquid (chicken broth works best, but water will do), then add the chicken. After 10 hours on low, use two forks to pull apart the chicken and mix ingredients together.

Butternut Squash Vegetable Stew

If you are looking to supercharge your stew by jamming it packed full of nutrients, this is your dish! Our stew is loaded to the brim with nutrient dense veggies, to bring you up to your optimum state of wellness. This is great for those days that you have a heavy lunch or if you are just looking for a light, but delicious dinner.

INGREDIENTS

1 pound of butternut squash, cubed

1 pound of carrots, chopped

2 onions, chopped

3 cloves of garlic, crushed

1 pound of cauliflower florets, chopped

DIRECTIONS

Caramelize your onions in a pan with some olive oil, ghee, or coconut oil. Once brown and soft, throw into your slow cooker with the squash, carrots, garlic, and cauliflower. A couple of bay leaves can add another layer of flavor if you have any lying around. Cook on low for 6-8 hours and enjoy a hearty stew that will nourish your body as much as it will taste amazing.

BBQ Pork Ribs

Who says you have to battle the flames of the BBQ to get a perfect set of ribs? These ribs will be so tender that they fall away from the bone in your mouth, but still have a little texture from the cartelization of the BBQ sauce when finished in the oven. Enjoy the tastiness of ribs without the work and fool all your friends in the process!

INGREDIENTS

3-4 pounds of baby back ribs

2 cloves of garlic, crushed

1 onion, chopped

1 small bottle of your favorite BBQ sauce

DIRECTIONS

Put in about ½ cup water in the bottom of the slow cooker along with the garlic and onion, but don't add the BBQ sauce just yet. After cooking on low for 8 hours, pull out the ribs and put them in an oven safe dish. Baste them with the BBQ sauce and put them in a pre-heated oven at 400 degrees for about ten minutes. This will caramelize the sauce, giving the ribs a bit of texture. Don't forget your napkin!

Beef Chili

Nobody walks away from a chili dinner still hungry! This hearty meal will fill you up quick and makes for great lunches and leftovers throughout the week. You can even pop your leftovers in the freezer for quick and easy meals whenever you find yourself in need.

INGREDIENTS

2 pounds ground beef

8 ounces tomato paste

3 TBSP chili powder

2 TBSP cumin

3 cloves crushed garlic

DIRECTIONS

Line the bottom of the slow cooker with the ground beef. In a small bowl mix the tomato paste, chili powder, cumin, and garlic with a little water. Once thoroughly mixed, pour the liquid over the meat and cook on low for 8-10 hours. After the cooking is complete, give the meat a firm stir to break up the large chunk into a more chili-like consistency.

Chapter 9: Cravings, Changes In The Body And Metabolic Adaptation

Probably the first noticeable event that will take place after you've begun your paleo diet is the increased frequency of cravings. Try to prepare yourself for this by anticipating cravings and having paleo-approved foods at the ready. It is often possible to 'trick' the brain into thinking the body has consumed one food, when really it has consumed another.

Beyond the cravings, some physiological changes will begin taking place starting at about the 1 week point. It's at this point that headaches might begin and general lethargy or loss of energy will occur. This is nothing to be alarmed about; it's completely normal and it's your body's method of readjusting itself to its new chemical and nutrient environment.

Because cutting out sugars and breads removes such a large source of carbohydrates from your diet, you will probably notice that you don't have as much physical energy to move heavy objects or sustain a cardiovascular workout for as long as you could have before the diet. Again, this is completely normal. This lack of energy is to be expected as your body switches its primary source of energy from carbohydrates (which are converted to glycogen) to fats (which will eventually be burned almost immediately as the body needs fuel).

To complete this 'switch', the liver has to function in a slightly different way. Ketones – used to convert fat to energy – become prevalent in the bloodstream and sometimes it can take a few weeks to fully engage this process within the body. Remember to be patient. It might also help to keep a log or journal of how you're feeling day-in and day-out, so that you can refer to these changes as indications that you are progressing along the paleo path.

Weight loss will be determined based on your body's metabolic rate combined with the amount of calories you consume while on the paleo diet. Someone who burns 2,500 calories every day just going about their daily business isn't going to lose weight if their caloric intake is 3,000 calories – even if those calories come from strictly paleo-friendly foods! This is the point about weight loss that seems lost on so many people: in order to burn fat, you must be in a state of caloric deficit.

While the paleo diet will aid in enhancing your body's methods for converting fat into energy, it will not be a silver bullet for weight loss unless you learn how to function at a caloric deficit. If at first you don't see the pounds coming off, and if that is your intended goal, don't get frustrated. Remind yourself that your body needs time and attention to do what it is you're making it do, and remember that the results you seek will come in time when you dedicate yourself to working the plan.

Another change that many paleo dieters report is an enhancement in their short-term memory and in their ability to focus. If you are someone who has a hard time maintaining attention during involved tasks, then trying the paleo diet might yield beneficial results. Because the human brain is such a complex system that reacts differently in everybody according to what foods we eat, it's difficult to know exactly how a paleo-specific diet will change the way we think. If any of the thousands of paleo diet anecdotes can be said to reflect reality, then it's very possible that eating from a strict, paleo-friendly menu could help with boosting brain power.

The final bodily change that may be noticeable for you is digestion. The simplicity of foods derived from the paleo diet means that your body will not have to work as hard to process them. Refined sugars, unsaturated fats and heavy foods like creams and cheeses can often cause stomach and intestinal problems – problems that, for some, disappear within only a few weeks of being on a paleo diet.

When it comes time to return to 'normal' food, the best advice is to go slow. Don't dive right back into eating starchy foods and sugary sweets. Slowly reintroduce the foods you used to eat and watch how your body reacts to them. After being on a paleo diet for a few weeks, you might find that suddenly you aren't as fond of candy!

Chapter 10: Snacking, Meal Preparation And Portioning

In between meals, it's inevitable that you're going to get hungry for foods other than what is approved by the paleo guidelines. The first important step to overcoming these urges is to acknowledge them for what they are when they present themselves. Often times, it helps to say to yourself, "This is an urge for _____ (bread, sugar, cheese, etc.). It is only an urge, and it will pass."

9 times out of 10, that's exactly what happens. The urge passes, although it's quite likely it will return in force before too long. Remember that when your body begins to crave a certain food, it's not a *requirement* that you comply with that urge. It is very possible that in depriving your system of the foods it is used to, you are causing it temporary discomfort as it is forced to adapt to this new nutritional scenario.

Be patient with your body and remember that you can still eat food – delicious food, even – but your focus remains on the approved list. In situations where you need to appease your stomach with *something* in between meals, consider choosing from the below list of paleo-friendly snacks:

- Kale chips

- Apple chips

- Zucchini chips

- Butternut chips

- Pumpkin seeds

- Olives

- Lettuce wraps

- Grilled peaches

- Pork rinds

- Honey dill carrots

- Walnuts

- Almonds

- Can of tuna

- Banana chips

- Jerky (beef, turkey, etc.)

- Dark chocolate

- Sardines

- Bacon

- Roasted chestnuts

- Frozen grapes

- Salami

- Frozen berries

Chapter 11: Easy Paleo Crock-Pot Breakfast Recipes

One of the challenges which many people new to paleo come across is what to have for breakfast. It is so easy just to grab cereals and milk, or throw bread into the toaster in the morning, particularly when we are rushing to get to work and get the kids to work.

It's also not always practical to cook a full breakfast with eggs or sausages every day, and you wouldn't necessarily want a cooked option every day in any case. This chapter aims to answer that dilemma with a whole load of easy recipes which all provide nutritious and tasty paleo breakfasts.

There are enough options here to meet all different taste varieties, and the recipes can all be carried out in the crock pot. I love the idea that you can put your breakfast on overnight and wake up in the morning to a delicious and healthy paleo meal waiting for you.

What better way to start your day than with a really nutritious breakfast, packed full of fruit if you opt for some of the apple choices. A nice puree with cinnamon makes a great breakfast choice whether its apple or pumpkin, and it also makes a great side dish so why not make a large batch and freeze some of it to have later with your main meal?

Crockpot Apple Breakfast Butter

If you have a sweet tooth, or just fancy a change from having eggs and meat for breakfast, try making this delicious apple breakfast butter. With the perfect combination of spices and the sweetness of the apples it works as a standalone dish, or you can use it as a sauce for other meals.

INGREDIENTS

Eight cups of chopped apples
Juice of a lemon
A tablespoon of cinnamon powder
A teaspoon of allspice
A teaspoon of clove
A teaspoon of ginger powder
Quarter of a teaspoon of ground nutmeg
One and a half cups of water
Half a cup of maple syrup

DIRECTIONS

Put all of the ingredients into the crock pot and set it to low. Leave to cook on low for eight hours, by which time the mixture should be brown and very soft. Leave it to cool and then transfer to a blender and puree until perfectly smooth. Pour into jars and keep in the fridge – it will last around two weeks.

Sweet Potato and Egg Skillet

INGREDIENTS
11-12 ounces of bacon, trim into 1-inch pieces
Coconut oil
4 ½ cups diced sweet potatoes
3 ½ cups diced zucchini or squash
1 cup diced yellow onion
1 chopped red bell pepper
6 large eggs, preferably free-range
A dash of pepper

DIRECTIONS

Heat a 12-inch cast-iron skillet over medium heat and cook your bacon strips until they are crispy. Remove the bacon from the pan leaving as much bacon fat in the bottom as possible. If there is not at least an eighth of an inch, add coconut oil to the pan to make up the difference. At this point, you want to turn your oven on and set to 400 degrees. Take your diced sweet potatoes and add them to your skillet, allowing the bottoms to brown without touching them. Once brown, stir them slightly until they are soft to the touch. Once softened add the rest of your vegetables and continue to cook until those are soft as well. Stir your bacon back in and mix until well blended. Create six holes in the mixture and break one egg in each hole. Place the entire skillet in the oven and heat for eight to thirteen minutes, or until the eggs are the desired consistency. Be careful when you remove the skillet from the oven it will be hot. Serves six.

Avocado Egg Bowls

INGREDIENTS

1 ripe avocado, cut in half and pit removed
1 whole egg
A pinch of salt
A dash of pepper
Other seasonings of your choice.

DIRECTIONS

Start by heating your oven to 425 degrees. You want to make your avocados stable so turn them over and cut enough of the skin so that they sit stably on the sheet. Turn each avocado over so that the meat is up and the hole is exposed. Put a pinch of salt in each hole of the avocado. In a small bowl whisk your egg until creamy and split between the two halves of the avocado. Season to your liking. Place the avocados in the oven for 15-17 minutes or until the egg consistency of your liking is achieved.

Sardine Egg Explosion

INGREDIENTS
1 can of sardines in oil or water
4 whole large eggs
2 tsp. parsley, chopped
1/4 yellow onion
2 garlic cloves, chopped

DIRECTIONS
Begin by placing a glass baking dish in your oven and preheat to 375 degrees. Use a fork and create flakes with your sardines and mix them with the parsley, onion, and garlic. Season with salt and pepper and place in the baking dish in the preheated oven. Cook for 5 minutes. Meanwhile, in a small dish, whisk your eggs until they are creamy. When the 5 minutes have passed, pull the dish out, pour the eggs over the sardines, season, and place back in the oven for 12 to 15 minutes or the eggs are well cooked. Makes 2 servings.

Rosemary Capered Eggs

INGREDIENTS
6 whole eggs
1 Tbsp. organic butter
2 Tbsp. capers
1 Tbsp. rosemary leaves
A pinch of salt

DIRECTIONS
In a small bowl, whisk together all six eggs until creamy. Heat a skillet on the stove, adding butter to melt. Once the butter starts to bubble, put the capers and rosemary in the pan and stir for 1-2 minutes. Pour the eggs into the skillet with the capers and cook on a low temperature as you would a scrambled egg. Season with a pinch of salt.

Summer Squash Breakfast

INGREDIENTS
6 summer squash
2 bunches of fresh asparagus
4 whole eggs
2 Tbsp. olive or coconut oil
A small bunch of pecans, chopped
A pinch of salt
A dash of pepper

DIRECTIONS

Fill a pan with three inches of water and bring to a simmer. Add the squash into the water and cook for 4 to 5 minutes, or until soft to the touch. Drain the water from the pan and then set aside until they are cool enough to handle. Put water in the same pan and heat to a simmer. Add the asparagus and the eggs, still in the shell, into the water. Cook for 5 to 9 minutes. Drain the water from the pan, place the eggs in cold water, and then peel and slice the eggs in half. Arrange the vegetables and eggs on your plate as desired, drizzle with the oil and season to taste.

Sweet Vanilla and Chia Treat

INGREDIENTS
1 ½ cups of Coconut milk
1/3 cup of black and white Chia seeds
3 Tbsp. all-natural Honey
1 tsp of pure Vanilla extract
A pinch of salt
Fresh fruit for layering
Unsweetened coconut flakes

DIRECTIONS
In an airtight container combine the coconut milk, chia, all-natural honey, pure vanilla extract, and a pinch of salt. Close the container and shake, or mix really well with spoon or whisk. Let sit in the refrigerator, overnight if possible. Serve as is or layer with your favorite fruits.

Blackberry Pineapple Smoothie

INGREDIENTS
1 large banana
1/4 cup chopped pineapple
1 cup of plain coconut milk
1 Tbsp. of coconut oil
1 Tbsp. of ground flax seed
2 cups frozen blackberries

DIRECTIONS
Cut all ingredients up into blend-able size. Combine all items
in blender and blend until smooth.

Crockpot Oatmeal with Squash

This breakfast is really nutritious combining the goodness of nuts, fruit, and spices with the sweetness of currants, coconut milk, and maple syrup, appealing to all taste buds and making a really great alternative to all the egg or meat-based paleo breakfast options. The oatmeal texture of the nuts makes it a really filling first meal of the day, guaranteed to boost your energy levels and set you up for a great morning.

INGREDIENTS

Half a cup of raw walnuts
Half a cup of raw almonds
One peeled and cut up butternut squash
Two diced apples with no peel
A teaspoon of cinnamon
Half a teaspoon of nutmeg
A tablespoon of coconut sugar
A cup of unsweetened Coconut milk

Toppings
Unsweetened Coconut milk
Dried or fresh currents
Unsweetened flaked coconut
Pure Maple syrup

DIRECTIONS

Take the raw nuts and soak them for 11 hours in filtered water. Once soaked, rinse them through and put into a processor and turn into a powder. Add this powder and all of the rest of the ingredients into the crock pot and cook on low for eight hours.

Use a potato masher to create the oatmeal consistency and top with your chosen topping before serving.

Crockpot frittata

If you fancy eggs for breakfast but with a difference then why not try this egg and vegetable frittata. The Italian seasoning brings out the flavor in the tomatoes creating a nice continental dish, perfect for a family weekend breakfast.

INGREDIENTS

Six eggs
Half a cup of non-dairy cheese
Four ounces of sliced mushrooms
A quarter of a cup of chopped spinach
A teaspoon of Italian seasoning
A teaspoon of salt
Half a teaspoon of pepper
A quarter of a cup of sliced cherry tomatoes
Two sliced onions
A teaspoon of ghee

DIRECTIONS

Use the ghee for frying up the vegetables for a few minutes in a pan and then putting them into the crock pot. Whisk the eggs, non-dairy cheese and seasonings together in a bowl before pouring over the vegetables in the crock pot. Cook it on high for 1-2 hours or on a low setting for 3-4 hours.

Apples Stuffed With Figs

For a real sweet treat to give you that energy boost first thing in the morning, try this apple and fig combination which is packed full of good nutrition and will keep you going right up to lunchtime.

INGREDIENTS

Five apples, cored
Five dried figs
A third of a cup of coconut sugar
A teaspoon of chopped crystallized ginger
A quarter of a cup of chopped pecans
A quarter of a teaspoon of nutmeg
Half a teaspoon of cinnamon
A teaspoon of lemon zest
Half a teaspoon of orange zest
A tablespoon of fresh lemon juice
A tablespoon of coconut oil
Half a cup of water
Half a teaspoon of cinnamon

DIRECTIONS

Remove the middle from each apple and set to one side. Combine all the stuffing ingredients together in a bowl and then spoon into each apple. Put the water into the crock pot and put the apples inside. Cook on high for an hour and a half.

Crockpot Apple Sauce

Another apple-focused dish, this sauce is perfect poured over whatever you fancy for breakfast, and also makes a great accompaniment to many of the pork meals in this book as well. Bonus!

INGREDIENTS

A third of a cup of cup coconut oil
A tablespoon of lemon juice
A quarter of a cup of evaporated cane juice
Half a teaspoon of cinnamon
A teaspoon of pure vanilla extract
Half a teaspoon of salt
Six peeled and cored apples, cubed

DIRECTIONS

Mix together the coconut oil, lemon juice, cinnamon powder, salt, vanilla extract and evaporated cane juice in a pan and heat together until the oil is completely melted. Put the apples into the crock pot and pour the melted mixture over them. Mix well until all the apples are coated and then cook on high for four hours.

Crock Pot Pulled Pork Breakfast

For the mornings when only meat will do, this pulled pork recipe is amazing. It can be made more breakfast-like if you serve it up with eggs or even an avocado, but it tastes delicious on its own. The spices really bring out the flavor in the meat and slow cooking it for so long means it will just fall apart on the fork once it's cooked. Invite the whole family round for a real breakfast treat, and you can always team it with the apple sauce for added sweetness.

INGREDIENTS

A 4-5 pound pork roast
Two tablespoons of chili powder
A tablespoon of cumin
A tablespoon of oregano
Two teaspoons of salt
A teaspoon of coriander
Two sliced onions

DIRECTIONS

Mix all of the spices together in a bowl and then rub the mixture over the meat. Put the onions into the bottom of the crockpot and put the seasoned meat on top. Cook for 8-10 hours on a low heat. Once cooked, shred the meat using a fork and stir the whole mixture together. Serve with avocados and a fried egg for a perfect breakfast, with a splash of hot sauce for added flavor. This dish freezes well so why not cook up a large batch and keep the rest.

Crock Pot Sweet Potato Breakfast Hash

The paleo alternative to hash browns, these vegetable-based hashes are really tasty and create a colorful and flavorsome addition to any meat-based cooked breakfast. They can be served on their own, but if you are looking for a cooked alternative to meat or eggs, then you can't go far wrong with these.

INGREDIENTS

One orange pepper
One yellow pepper
100 grams of butternut squash
300 grams of sweet potato
Two diced tomatoes
Two tablespoons of coconut oil
A teaspoon of garlic puree
A teaspoon of thyme
A teaspoon of mustard powder

DIRECTIONS

Dice all of the vegetables, add the seasoning and coconut oil and put it all into the crockpot. Cook on low for four hours or on high for two and a half hours.

Crockpot Breakfast Pie

This delicious dish combines three fantastic breakfast ingredients in one amazing dish – sausages, eggs, and vegetables – what more could you ask for! It's also a versatile dish you could adapt to use as a family evening meal if need be but definitely an ideal lazy Sunday morning big breakfast!

INGREDIENTS

Eight whisked eggs
A shredded sweet potato (plus your choice of vegetables)
A pound of chopped up pork sausage
A diced onion
A tablespoon of garlic powder
Two teaspoons of basil

DIRECTIONS

Shred all of the vegetables and then add all of the ingredients into the crockpot together. Put the setting on low and cook for between 6-8 hours to make sure the pork is cooked through.

Crockpot Breakfast Casserole

This casserole features the goodness of kale, mixed with the comfort of eggs and sausages and creates a really nutritious start to the morning. The garlic and leek create really strong flavors in this filling dish which will be a hit with everyone.

INGREDIENTS

Two tablespoons of coconut oil
One and three-quarter cups of sliced leek
Two teaspoons of chopped garlic
A cup of kale
Eight eggs
Two-thirds of a cup of sweet potato, peeled and grated
One and a half cups of beef sausage

DIRECTIONS

Melt the coconut oil in a pan and saute the leeks, kale and garlic. Mix the sautéed vegetables with the eggs, sausage and sweet potato and put it all into the crock pot. Cook on a low heat for six hours.

Crock Pot Paleo Mexican Breakfast

For breakfast with added kick, why not try this Mexican-spiced casserole to really get you up and going first thing in the morning! It's not one for the faint-hearted but if you fancy something a bit different, then why not go for it – it's particularly good if you have a really big day ahead of you and maybe won't have time for lunch later.

INGREDIENTS

One cubed sweet potato
Eight whisked eggs
Half a pound of turkey bacon
A chopped onion
A chopped pepper
An eight-ounce pack of mushrooms, chopped

Half a pack of Mexican seasoning
Guacamole, salsa, and jalapeno to garnish

DIRECTIONS

Fry the turkey bacon in a pan until crispy. Leave it to one side to cool down and crumble it when ready. Cook the onions in the pan. Put all of the remaining ingredients into the crockpot and stir well. Cook on a low heat for 6-8 hours and then serve with the spicy garnish options.

Crock Pot Sausage and Egg Breakfast

This breakfast features healthy broccoli for a nutritious kick start, and sausage to make it nice and filling, giving you the energy to take you through the rest of the day. Make sure you choose a tasty non-dairy cream alternative to add to the creamy flavor of this wonderful dish.

INGREDIENTS

A chopped head of broccoli
A 12-ounce pack of sausages, cooked and sliced
A cup of grated non-dairy cheese
Ten eggs
Three-quarters of a cup of non-dairy cream alternative
Two crushed garlic cloves
Half a teaspoon of salt
A quarter of a teaspoon of pepper

DIRECTIONS

Layer half of the broccoli, sausage, and non-dairy cheese into the crockpot and then repeat to create a second layer. Mix together all of the rest of the ingredients in a bowl and then pour over the layers. Cook on low for 4-5 hours or on high for 2-3 hours.

Crockpot Breakfast Egg Casserole

This casserole is the perfect start for a big day ahead and can be cooked overnight, so it's ready for the whole family to enjoy on a lazy day at the weekend. It's very filling, and the bacon adds a nice salty flavor to break up the eggs and yams with a strong savory kick.

INGREDIENTS

A pound of cooked, chopped bacon
One diced onion
One diced pepper
One tablespoon of coconut oil
Two grated yams
Two grated garlic cloves
A dozen eggs
One cup of coconut milk
A teaspoon of dill

DIRECTIONS

Grease the crock pot and then melt the coconut oil in a pan and cook the onion, garlic, and pepper until soft. Layer a third of the sweet potato in the crock pot followed by a third of the onion mixture and a third of the bacon. Repeat until all of the ingredients are in the pot. Mix the eggs, coconut milk and seasoning together and pour over the layers in the crock pot. Cook on a low heat for 8-10 hours.

Hopefully this chapter has given you tons of ideas for interesting breakfasts and has broken the paleo cycle of sausage and egg every day. With choices ranging from apple and pumpkins, through to oatmeal alternative, you will be able to select a great tasting breakfast daily.

With a crockpot the best thing is you can throw the ingredients in before you go up to bed and let it cook on low overnight, knowing that when you get up in the morning and have kids to sort out, school run to prepare for and your work outfit to get ready, you have one less thing to worry about as breakfast is just there ready to be served.

Whether it's a quick bowl of puree as you rush out the door, or a lazy Sunday with the whole family indulging in a breakfast casserole, there is something here for everyone to enjoy.

Chapter 12 – Easy Paleo After-Work Recipes

If you work hard during the day, the last thing you want to do when you get home is start preparing a meal and cooking for everyone. This is the joy of owning a crock pot. You can cook over the weekend and then heat it up when you get home.

You can cook a big portion and freeze it all, so you just need to put it in the microwave when you get home. Or you can put it all on in the morning and leave it on a low heat for around eight hours, so it's all ready and waiting for you when you get home.

Whichever way you use your crockpot it will save you time, save you washing up and is also incredibly simple as you generally don't need to do any prior preparation, just put all of the ingredients into the crockpot and stir it up, before turning it on.

They also have the added bonus of taking up a lot less energy than a conventional oven, so your bills should be reduced as well, and they are safe to leave for hours without having to continually check, stir, top up or add to.

Just because you have come home a little late, your only option needn't be to dial an unhealthy take away because you haven't got time. Just plan a little ahead with these meals, and you could end up with a delicious, healthy curry or a hearty stew ready and waiting for you when you get home from a hard day's work.

Lettuce Crockpot Tacos

These are great healthy and paleo alternative to traditional tacos, using the lettuce leaves to form the taco shell rather than the corn-based version. They are full of flavor and a really crispy crunchy lettuce leaf around the chicken really does add to the texture and flavor, creating a natural and more healthy taco crunch.

INGREDIENTS

Two breasts of chicken
Two fresh tomatoes
Two onions
Two garlic cloves
One tablespoon of honey
One teaspoon of basil
A teaspoon of chili powder
A teaspoon of cloves
Three tablespoons of water
Lettuce leaves, crunchy

DIRECTIONS

Cut up the onions, tomatoes and garlic cloves. Put all of the ingredients apart from the lettuce, into the crock pot. Cook on low for six hours. Once cooked, shred the chicken and mix it all together. Use the lettuce leaves as tacos and serve with salad.

Crock Pot Ribs with Ginger

These sticky sweet ribs are a real treat to all the meat lovers out there and prove that paleo doesn't mean you can't enjoy a sweet treat every now and then. They are really flavorsome and the anise and ginger really bring out the meat in this creative recipe.

INGREDIENTS

A short beef rib
Two red onions
Two crushed garlic cloves
1 teaspoon of ground ginger
Two-star anise
A tablespoon of honey

DIRECTIONS

Put all of the ingredients into the crock pot and add an inch depth of water into the bottom of the pot. Cook for around six to eight hours. Once ready, serve with vegetables.

Crock Pot Beef with Kale

This hearty dish is perfect for the whole family and makes a great Sunday roast dinner alternative to chicken if you are looking for a change. The kale creates a nice strong and nutritious addition to the beef, and really complements the flavor. Team with sweet carrots to balance it all out.

INGREDIENTS

Fourteen ounces of beef steak cut into cubes

Two chopped onions
Two chopped carrots
Half a chopped celeriac
Half a chopped swede
Six cloves of garlic
Water
Four handfuls of kale

DIRECTIONS

Add two inches of water to the crock pot and then put all of the ingredients, apart from the kale, into the crock pot. Set it to cook for six hours. Just before the six hours is up, put the kale on the top and steam them for 5 to 10 minutes.

Crock Pot Chili Chicken

This spicy dish is perfect for a paleo dinner party with friends and family and has a really good kick to the flavor. You can increase the chili powder amount to suit the level of intensity which you want to achieve.

INGREDIENTS

Eight to twelve chicken thighs, boned and skinned
A 16-ounce jar of salsa
A 16-ounce tin of tomatoes
A chopped onion
A chopped pepper
Two tablespoons of chili powder

DIRECTIONS

Chop the chicken, and put everything into the crock pot together and stir all the ingredients together well until the chicken is thoroughly coated. Cook the crock pot on high for four to six hours, or on low for six to eight hours. It tastes better the longer you cook it for.

Crock Pot Roast Chicken Dinner

If you have all the family round for a roast dinner then there is no need to use the over and heat up the whole kitchen, the crock pot can solve that problem, and the result is just as great, with wonderful flavors. It can also cook well in advance bringing in that added convenience, not to mention the lack of washing up after!

INGREDIENTS

A whole chicken
One onion
One bulb of garlic
A lemon
A tablespoon of paprika
A teaspoon of sea salt
A teaspoon of pepper
A teaspoon of thyme
Eight inches of kitchen twine
Two carrots

DIRECTIONS

Put the carrots on the bottom of the crock pot. Untie the chicken and remove the giblets. Stuff the chicken carcass with all of the ingredients and then use the twine to tie the legs together again, so it all stays in place. Sprinkle the paprika on top of the chicken, so it will look browned when it comes out of the crock pot. Put the crock pot on high and cook it for four hours. You can serve it as a Sunday lunch or shred it and keep it in the fridge to use throughout the week for a number of meals.

Crockpot Paleo Chicken

This crockpot chicken dish has an amazing Italian flavor and provides a great alternative, proving that paleo doesn't mean bland meat dishes, you can still experience and enjoy great traditional tastes.

INGREDIENTS

Two tablespoons of coconut oil
A large chopped onion
A quarter of a cup of tomato paste
One and a half teaspoons of dried oregano
Two to three crushed cloves of garlic
A quarter of a teaspoon of red pepper flakes
A tin of tomatoes
Half a cup of chicken stock
Two pounds of chopped mushrooms

DIRECTIONS

Cook the coconut oil, oregano, onions, garlic, tomato paste and red pepper flakes in a saucepan and then put the mixture into the crockpot. Add in the chicken stock, tomatoes, and mushrooms, and then place the chicken pieces into the mixture as well. Mix it all together and cook on a low heat for four to six hours.

Delectable Broccoli Soup

INGREDIENTS
4 pieces of bacon, diced
1 yellow onion, chopped
1 clove of garlic, minced
1 large head of fresh broccoli, chopped
4 cups of low-sodium chicken broth
1 cup of unsweetened coconut milk
A pinch of salt
A dash of pepper

DIRECTIONS
In a large pot over medium heat, cook your bacon until it is crisp. Take the bacon from the pan but leave the bacon fat in the bottom of the pot. Combine the onion and garlic and cook over medium heat in the leftover bacon fat. Once those are soft and slightly translucent add the broccoli and cook, stirring, for two minutes. Add the chicken broth to the pan, bring to a boil, and then lower the heat to low and simmer for nine to ten minutes, or until the broccoli is tender. Put the soup, in batches, into your blender and puree until smooth. Put the soup back into the pot, add the coconut milk, and stir. Season to taste.

Beef and Kale Salad

INGREDIENTS
8 cups of baby kale, kale greens without stems, or salad mixture
2 cups roasted yellow squash, sweet potatoes, or a combination of both
2 apples cored and sliced
1/4 cup of fresh Pomegranate seeds
1 ¼ lbs cooked and sliced beef

Dressing
1/2 cup of olive oil
Juice from one large orange
2 tsp Apple Cider vinegar
1 tsp raw Dijon mustard
1 tsp raw, all-natural honey
1/8 tsp ground cloves
A pinch of salt
A dash of pepper

DIRECTIONS
To create your salad, take all ingredients and combine in a large bowl. Toss accordingly. To create your dressing, put all ingredients in a glass container with lid, and shake until properly combined and well blended.

Meatballs and Greens

INGREDIENTS
2 Tbsp. extra-virgin olive oil
2 Tbsp. of Italian blended seasonings
2 garlic cloves, chopped
1/4 cup coconut flour
A dash of Paprika
A pinch of salt
1 ½ lbs grass-fed ground beef
1 yellow onion, chopped finely

Greens:
4 pieces of bacon, chopped
1 bunch of collard greens chopped, with stems removed
1 bunch of swiss chard chopped
1 cup of low-sodium Chicken broth
2 tsp Apple Cider vinegar
 A pinch of salt
A dash of pepper

DIRECTIONS
Begin by heating your oven to 400 degrees. In a medium bowl place your beef, garlic, onion, coconut flour, and spices and mix to coat beef. Create, you're your hands, 2-3 inch meatballs and place them on a baking sheet covered with baking paper. Brush the meatballs with olive oil and sprinkle your Italian spices over them. Bake for 25-35 minutes, or until baked completely through.
To create your greens first start by cooking your bacon in a deep skillet until it begins to get crispy. Toss in the greens and stir until they are coated in the bacon fat. Add your low-sodium chicken broth and simmer for 10-12 minutes or until

the greens are tender.

Vegetable Noodles with Cream Sauce

INGREDIENTS
2 Tbsp. extra virgin olive oil
1 tsp sea salt
2 medium zucchini

Sauce
2 Tbsp. extra virgin olive oil
3 cups of low sodium chicken stock
3 cups of fresh or frozen but thawed cauliflower tops
1/2 cup unsweetened coconut milk
4 cloves of garlic, chopped
A pinch of salt.
A dash of pepper

DIRECTIONS
Using either a spiralizer or carrot peeler, slice the zucchini into noodles. Carefully lay each noodle on paper towels and sprinkle with a pinch of salt. Let the noodles stand for ten to twelve minutes. Squeeze the water from the noodles after this time and cook on medium for a couple of minutes, just until warm.

To make the sauce, you will start by heating oil in a skillet and adding the garlic once hot. Cook the garlic for a couple of minutes and then remove the skillet from the heat. In a separate saucepan combine the broth and the cauliflower, bring to a boil, and cook for 8 to 9 minutes. Drain the cauliflower but keep the liquid. You want to put the cooked cauliflower and garlic into a blender. Add half of the broth you reserved, the coconut milk, salt, and pepper. Blend the ingredients until they are smooth and the consistency is correct. You may add more broth if it is needed. Top the zucchini noodles with the sauce and serve.

Creamy Cod with Pesto

INGREDIENTS

For Pesto
2 ½ cups of Arugula
3 Tbsp. of sliced almonds
Juice of a ½ of a lemon
1/4 cup extra-virgin olive oil
 A pinch of salt

For Fish
2 Tbsp. of almond grounds
2 Tbsp. of fresh pesto
6 oz. of fresh Cod
A pinch of salt

For Noodles
2 Tbsp. extra-virgin olive oil
1 zucchini cut into pasta with carrot peeler or spiralizer
1/4 cup of fresh pesto
A pinch of salt
1/2 cup Cherry tomatoes (halved)

DIRECTIONS

Begin by heating your oven to 350 degrees. Using either a spiralizer or carrot peeler, slice the zucchini into noodles. Carefully lay each noodle on paper towels and sprinkle with a pinch of salt. Let the noodles stand for ten to twelve minutes. Squeeze the water from the noodles after this time and cook on medium for a couple of minutes, just until warm.

Put 2 tablespoons of almonds into a food processor and create grounds, setting aside for later. Put all ingredients for pest into the food processor and process on high until well blended and smooth. Set the pesto aside. In a separate bowl take 2 tablespoons of the almond grounds and 2 tablespoons of the pesto and combine them. Using a paper towel get all moisture off of your cod and place it on a baking sheet. Put a pinch of salt over the cod and then spoon your pesto mixture on top of the fish, creating a crust for it. Put your fish in the preheated oven and bake it for 9 to 11 minutes.

During the fishes cooking process heat oil in a large skillet and add your noodles and a quarter of a cup of your pesto. Use the rest of the pesto if it is almost gone. Sauté the noodles for 4 to 5 minutes or until they are tender and season to taste. Place the fish on top of the noodles and sprinkle the cherry tomatoes over the top.

Chicken Lettuce Taco Wraps

INGREDIENTS

1 lb of lean chicken tenders cut into one-inch strips
1 yellow onion, chopped
1 clove of garlic, minced
1 orange pepper, chopped
6-7 diced white mushrooms
3 stalks of celery, chopped
3 carrots, sliced
6-7 Brussels sprouts that have stems removed and are cut in quarters
2 tsp Rice vinegar
1 Tbsp. of Coconut amino
1 tsp of crushed red pepper
A pinch of salt
A dash of pepper
2 Tbsp. of coconut oil
1 head of lettuce with the leaves separated

DIRECTIONS
In a large pan, heat your oil over medium heat. Once hot add your onions, pepper, garlic, and celery and saute for 3 to 4 minutes. The onion should look translucent. Place your chicken in the skillet with the vegetables and continue cooking for 5 to 6 more minutes, or until the chicken begins to brown. Stir occasionally to keep from burning. Once the chicken is cooked, add in your Brussel sprouts, carrots, and mushrooms and cook for another 4 minutes, stirring constantly. Next stir in the vinegar, amino, ginger, and red peppers and stir until everything is coated. Continue cooking for another few minutes, or until the chicken is fully cooked.

Place a spoonful of the filling in the lettuce leaf and eat like a taco.

Crockpot Paleo Stew

This rich beef stew provides a real hearty warming and filling dish, a perfect comfort food for cold winter nights, or serve it with a salad in the summer, whichever suits you! It's paleo perfection in a pot! You won't even notice there are no potatoes in it.

INGREDIENTS

Two pounds of stewing beef
Two cups of beef stock
A teaspoon of vinegar
A chopped onion
Two chopped celery stalks
Two chopped carrots
Crushed cloves of garlic – two
A teaspoon of paprika
Three bay leaves
Half a teaspoon of salt
Half a teaspoon of black pepper
Half a teaspoon of dried rosemary
A tablespoon of arrowroot powder

DIRECTIONS

Put all of the ingredients into the crockpot apart from the arrowroot powder. Cook it on low for eight hours. Just before it's ready, ladle all of the liquid out into a saucepan and bring it to the boil. Add in the arrowroot powder to thicken it up. Once ready, pour it back over the mixture and serve.

Crock Pot Lamb Stew

Moving away from chicken and beef, why not have a go at this Moroccan inspired lamb stew with its distinctive flavors and spices. We guarantee that everyone will love it and forget that it's even a paleo dish. It's great served with a natural paleo tabbouleh to really finish off that Moroccan feel.

INGREDIENTS

Two pounds of diced lamb
Four tablespoons of Moroccan spice mix
Two chopped sweet potatoes
One diced pepper
One cup of chopped apricots
A tin of tomatoes
Three tablespoons of coconut oil

DIRECTIONS

Put the spice mixture into a frying pan and cook, add in the lamb and coat it in the spices. Add the coconut oil and stir together. Then put all of the ingredients into your crock pot and cook it on low for seven hours. Serve with cauliflower tabbouleh.

Crockpot Apples and Cabbage

The sweetness of the apples combined with the tart mustard and cabbage creates a really interesting combination for this dish. Serve it up alongside your classic meat dish or have it as a standalone vegetable option – it all depends how hungry you are! Either way, it's a nutritious dish full of vitamins and great energy boosting ingredients.

INGREDIENTS

Two tart-flavoured apples
One chopped cabbage
One chopped onion
Half a teaspoon of salt
An eighth of a teaspoon of freshly ground pepper
Half a cup of chicken stock
A cup of apple juice
Three tablespoons of mustard
Coconut oil

DIRECTIONS

Put everything into the crock pot and mix it all together, so it is all really well combined. Cook it on a low heat for six to eight hours and stir it every couple of hours to make sure it's all combined. Once ready, serve and eat immediately.

Paleo Spicy Soup

This pumpkin curry soup is really simple, using only five ingredients and provides a really filling and spicy meal for everyone. The flavor combination is perfect for a cold winter's day, or for a quick lunch perhaps with some salad on the side.

INGREDIENTS

A kilogram of pumpkin

A can of coconut milk
Two teaspoons of curry powder
A teaspoon of salt
Two teaspoons of pepper
Coconut oil

DIRECTIONS

Put all of the ingredients into the crock pot and stir several times to make sure the pumpkin is coated with all the spices. Pour the coconut milk over the mixture and add water to cover it. Cook it on low for six to eight hours.

Crock Pot Vegetable Curry

This wonderfully creamy vegetable korma is perfectly paleo with no added sugars or oils and depending on how spicy you want to make it, it can really pack a good punch. It's a really flavorsome dish and makes a nice alternative to eating meat all the time on the paleo regime.

INGREDIENTS

A large cauliflower in florets
Two chopped carrots
A cup of chopped green beans
Half a chopped onion
Two crushed garlic cloves
Three-quarters of a can of coconut milk
Two teaspoons of curry powder
A teaspoon of salt

A teaspoon of garam marsala
A teaspoon of red pepper flakes
Two teaspoons of almond meal

INSTRUCTIONS

Put all of the vegetables, onion, and garlic into the crock pot
and mix them together well. Take a bowl and mix together the
milk, salt, flakes, garam masala and curry powder together and
stir well. Pour the combined liquid into the crock pot and
sprinkle the almond meal over the top. Cook it on a low heat
for eight hours until it takes on a thick consistency and serve
immediately.

Crockpot Roast – Mississippi style

This spicy chicken dish will be a real showstopper for a special
dinner party or special occasion with family and friends. The
seasoning and chili really bring out the chicken flavor with a
strong Mississippi kick, and it is guaranteed to be loved by
everyone. Serve it with a nice cooling salad with crunchy
lettuce to balance out the strong chili flavors. You can make it
as hot or as mild as your guests will stand by adding in extra
jalapenos or serving it with a spicy salsa.

INGREDIENTS

Five and a half pounds of roast chicken
Four tablespoons of ranch seasoning
A cup of beef stock

A tablespoon of coconut amino

Ten chili peppers

Three tablespoons of ghee

INSTRUCTIONS

Put the meat into the crockpot and pour the stock over it. Sprinkle the seasoning over the meat and then drizzle it with the coconut. Put the chili peppers around the meat in the crockpot and the ghee on top of it. Cook it on a low heat and leave it to cook for eight hours. Once ready, shred the meat with a fork to make it ready to eat.

Crockpot Pork Ramen

This amazing ramen dish replaces traditional noodles with spiralized courgettes to make it a true paleo dish full of flavor but still retaining that traditional feel to this Thai-inspired dish. The combination of pork, chicken, and fish really work well together to create a truly flavorsome ramen concoction that the whole family will be requesting on a regular basis.

INGREDIENTS

Two and a half pounds of pork

Four cups of chicken soup

Half a cup of coconut amino

A quarter of a cup of rice vinegar

A quarter of a cup of fish sauce

Two tablespoons of chili garlic sauce

A tablespoon of fresh ginger

Juice of a lime

A tablespoon of Chinese 5-spice

Two cups of baby portabellas

A spiralized courgette

A teaspoon of salt

A teaspoon of pepper

Spice blend:

A teaspoon of cinnamon

A teaspoon of lemon pepper

A teaspoon of star anise seeds

Half a teaspoon of fennel

A quarter of a teaspoon of cloves

DIRECTIONS

Put the pork into the crockpot and add in all of the ingredients except the mushrooms and courgettes. Cook it on low for seven hours. Once the time is nearly up, remove the pork and shred it. Return it to the crockpot with the mushrooms and courgette and cook for another 10 minutes until the mushrooms are soft.

Crockpot Chicken with Apple

This simple dish is a twist on the traditional pork with apple sauce and brings out the flavors of the onion and the garlic. The apple sauce really adds to the moisture of the chicken dish and the cinnamon creates a sincere warmth to the dish, making it a lovely warming meal that all the family will enjoy.

INGREDIENTS

Four chicken breasts
Two cups of apple sauce
Half a teaspoon of onion powder
Half a teaspoon of garlic powder
A quarter of a teaspoon of black pepper
Quarter of a teaspoon of cinnamon

DIRECTIONS

Put the chicken into the crockpot and cover with the apple sauce and the spices before cooking on low for around seven hours. Make sure the chicken is thoroughly cooked through before serving.

Crock Pot Chicken Salsa

This is a really simple and perfect mid-week dinner for all the family with only a few ingredients and a nice spicy flavor to please everyone. It just takes a few handfuls of ingredients thrown into the crockpot and produces a really wonderful aroma while cooking.

INGREDIENTS

Four chicken breasts
A 16-ounce jar of salsa
A third of a cup of water
One and a half tablespoons of parsley
Half a tablespoon of cilantro
A teaspoon of onion powder
A teaspoon of garlic powder
Half a tablespoon of oregano
Half a teaspoon of paprika
Half a teaspoon of cumin
A teaspoon of chili powder
A quarter of a teaspoon of pepper

DIRECTIONS

Put the chicken into the bottom of the crock pot and then add the rest of the ingredients and mix together well. Cook on a low heat for around six hours and make sure the chicken is cooked through completely before serving.

Crock Pot Squash with Rosemary

This vegetarian option gives paleo eaters an alternative evening meal to all of the meat dishes and the vinegar and rosemary really increase the flavors of this dish which works well on its own or as a side dish.

INGREDIENTS

One squash
Half a cup of vegetable stock

Two tablespoons of coconut oil
A tablespoon of balsamic vinegar
A teaspoon of salt
A teaspoon of pepper
Three tablespoons of rosemary
Three cloves of garlic

DIRECTIONS

Cut the squash in half and scoop out the seeds before slicing each half into four pieces and put into the crock pot. Pour the stock into the crock pot and then drizzle the squash slices with the oil and vinegar. Sprinkle the garlic and rosemary over the slices and cook on low for 7-8 hours.

Hopefully, all of these dishes have inspired you to see just how quick and easy it can be to create wonderful flavorsome meals for the whole family using a crockpot, while still maintaining a strict paleo routine.

Taking various combinations of meats, vegetables, and different spices means you can still develop wonderfully creative options with inspiration drawn from Italy, Morocco and India, to name but a few.

Paleo does not have to be hard, or bland and using the crock pot means you can create really quick and easy meals, by just combining the ingredients, mixing them up and leaving them to cook by themselves.

I love that I don't have to check every five minutes, or worry that the pan is boiling over, or boiling dry. There is no need to keep stirring regularly or to stand over the cooker waiting for it to be ready. The crock pot means I can throw everything in, first thing in the morning, go out all day with the family or to work, and come home knowing a wonderful dinner is there waiting for us.

It's a small thing, but I also love that there is so little washing up to do after a meal now. Instead of numerous bowls, pots and pans and instruments used to prepare all the ingredients beforehand, all I really end up washing is a knife, chopping board, and the inner crock pot bowl, and that's really it. It really is a wonderful time saver.

Chapter 13: Easy Paleo Dessert Recipes

Just because you have to cut back on refined sugar and butter and dairy, doesn't mean you can't create amazing paleo desserts and best of all you can use your slow cooker to produce them cutting back on time and preparation.

Check out all of these amazing dessert recipes to make sure you don't miss out on all things sweet while maintaining your healthy paleo outlook. From apples to nuts and maple syrup, from non-dairy chocolate to slow cooker fudge, you will be amazed at what you can create on a paleo regime and with your crock pot.

All of the family can enjoy these wonderful desserts together, and it's so easy to just throw the ingredients in and leave them to cook while you are enjoying your dinner together, saving time and washing up after.

Glazed Crock Pot Pecans

This delicious nutty dessert is so simple to make and so effective – be warned that once tasted they can become quite addictive! The nutty and sweet flavors combine really well together creating a delicious little pot of goodness that everyone will enjoy over and over again.

INGREDIENTS

Three cups of raw pecans
A quarter of a cup of maple syrup
Two teaspoons of ground vanilla beans
A teaspoon of salt
A teaspoon of coconut oil

DIRECTIONS

Put all of the ingredients into the crock pot and cook on a low level for 1-3 hours. Leave to cool and store in a jar once ready.

Apple Puree

This delicious puree makes an amazing zingy dessert packed full of vitamin C, the perfect quick and easy follow-up to a big meal. The cinnamon adds a really good spicy flavor, the perfect combination! It really levels out the sweetness of the apples. A classically simple dessert that everyone will enjoy.

INGREDIENTS

Three crock pot's worth of apples, cored and chopped into chunks
Two cups of water
Two sticks of cinnamon
A few tablespoons of ground cinnamon

DIRECTIONS

Fill up the crock pot with apples and the water and add in the cinnamon sticks. Put the rest of the apples in the fridge for now. Turn the crock pot up to high and cook for six hours. Reduce the heat to medium and stir the apples. Add in more apples as the mixture will have reduced. Cook again for another 5-6 hours. Keep repeating this method until all the apples have been cooked. It should take around 24 hours altogether.

Once it's all cooked, remove the cinnamon sticks and stir in the ground cinnamon into the mixture. Use a blender to finally create the smooth consistency of butter. Spoon it into jars and keep in the fridge. It should last around three weeks in the fridge, and it can also be frozen if you wish.

Quinoa and Apple Crock Pot

This dessert has a real holiday flavor to it and makes a great addition to a Christmas or Thanksgiving Paleo meal if you are looking for a special sweet pudding to mark the occasion. The maple syrup and cinnamon really combine well with the apple flavors in this unusual dessert.

INGREDIENTS

A cup of quinoa
Two cups of coconut milk
A teaspoon of vanilla extract
One small apple, cut into cubes
Half a cup of unsweetened apple sauce
Two tablespoons of maple syrup
Two teaspoons of ground cinnamon

DIRECTIONS

Put all of the ingredients into the crockpot and cook it on low for eight hours. Simple!

Pumpkin puree

This delicious puree gives an alternative option to apples but still provides a really sweet dessert option, and the port flavor provides a nice kick to it while maintaining the sweetness. It can be enjoyed on its own or even used as a sauce for a main meat dish due to its slight savory peppery flavors.

INGREDIENTS

Two 15 ounce tins of pumpkin
Half a cup of ruby port
A cup of coconut sugar
A quarter of a cup of maple syrup
A vanilla bean
A pinch of black pepper
A pinch of cayenne pepper
A tablespoon of cinnamon

DIRECTIONS

Put all of the ingredients apart from the cinnamon, into the crockpot and cook it on high heat for three hours. Take the lid off and stir in the cinnamon and then cook on high heat for half an hour with the lid left off. It should achieve a thick caramel consistency. Continue cooking and stirring until you are happy with the consistency.

Crock Pot Apple Pie Sauce

Continuing with the puree/sauce dessert theme, this recipe takes the traditional apple puree dessert one step further with the extra flavors which give it that special kick. It's perfect as a dessert or as a sauce with other dishes, including pork.

INGREDIENTS

A third of a cup of coconut oil
A tablespoon of lemon juice
A quarter of a cup of evaporated cane juice
Half a teaspoon of cinnamon
A teaspoon of vanilla extract
Half a teaspoon of salt
Six apples cut into cubes

DIRECTIONS

Cook all of the ingredients apart from the apples, in a small pan together and mix until the coconut oil is melted. Place all of the apples into the crock pot and then pour the mixture over them. Mix it all together and then cook on a high heat for four hours.

Non-chocolate paleo cookies

A real non-dairy treat, why should paleo mean no chocolate?! These are really simple and easy to make, and taste absolutely delicious. Just make sure to choose a really good quality non-dairy chocolate for these, and the combination of almond and chocolate flavors will make them irresistible. Make sure you don't overcook them – they are better slightly on the gooey side as they will harden a lot as they cool down.

INGREDIENTS

A quarter of a cup of melted coconut oil
A cup of coconut sugar
A large egg white

Half a teaspoon of vanilla extract
One and a half cups of ground almonds
One and three-quarters of a teaspoon of baking powder
Half a teaspoon of salt
Half a cup of non-dairy chocolate chips

DIRECTIONS

Line your crockpot with parchment paper. Mix all of the ingredients together in a bowl until well combined and create a dough from it. Put the dough into the crock pot and press down. Cook on a low heat for about 2 hours, until the outside is golden brown. Try not to overcook. Gently remove from the crockpot and leave to cool down completely before cutting into cookies.

Crock Pot Spicy Pears

For a really fruity end to an evening meal, these spicy, perfect pears will definitely create a wonderful dessert to finish off any paleo evening meal. They can be created quickly and easily for a straight forward pudding, or why not jazz them up for a paleo dinner party with all of your friends.

INGREDIENTS

Five medium ripe pears
Two cups of fresh orange juice
A quarter of a cup of maple syrup
Five cardamom pods
A cinnamon stick

Ginger cut into slices

DIRECTIONS

Peel the pears and slice them across the bottom so they can stand up straight. Core the pears and put them standing upright in the crockpot. Pour the liquid on top of each pear and put all of the ingredients in the crockpot. Cook on a low heat and cook for 3-4 hours. Every hour cover the pears with more of the juice. Check the pears are soft when the cooking time is over.

Non-Dairy Chocolate Cake

This low carb paleo chocolate cake is amazing and can all be made in your own crock pot, saving on cooking energy as well as containing no sugar or dairy – challenge your family to tell the difference! As long as you choose good quality non-dairy chocolate, it will be amazing.

INGREDIENTS

One and a half cups of almond flour
Three-quarters of a cup of sweetener
Two-thirds of a cup of non-dairy cocoa powder alternative
Three-quarters of a cup of protein powder
Two teaspoons of baking powder
A quarter of a teaspoon of salt
Half a cup of melted coconut oil
Four large eggs
Three-quarters of a cup of coconut milk

One teaspoon of vanilla extract
Half a cup of non-dairy sugar-free chocolate chips

DIRECTIONS

Mix together the sweetener, almond flour, non-dairy cocoa powder, baking powder, protein powder and salt in a bowl. Then add the coconut oil, eggs, milk and vanilla and mix it all together, with the non-dairy chocolate chips. Pour the mixture into your crockpot and cook on a low heat for three hours. Turn off and leave it to cool for 20 minutes before serving.

Crock Pot Pear Crumble

This is a wonderful paleo version of a traditional pear crumble, using maple syrup and coconut sugar to provide the sweetness, balanced out with the nutmeg and cinnamon spices to create a really wonderful dessert the whole family will fall in love with.

INGREDIENTS

Six firm pears halved or quartered
A quarter of a cup of maple syrup
Half a cup of water
Half a teaspoon of cinnamon
Half a teaspoon of ginger
A quarter of a teaspoon of nutmeg
A teaspoon of vanilla extract

Topping
Two-thirds of a cup rolled oats
A teaspoon of coconut oil

Two teaspoons of coconut sugar
One teaspoon of maple syrup

DIRECTIONS

Put all of the initial ingredients (not the topping) into the
crock pot together and cook on high for one hour, before
turning it down to low and cooking for a further three hours.
Then put all of this into a baking tin. Combine the topping
ingredients together in a blender, then sprinkle over the pear
mixture and bake in the oven for half an hour to make the
topping crunchy.

Fudge Without Dairy

This really is a delicious alternative to the traditional style
fudge – just don't leave it out too long in room temperature as
it will become soft and sticky quicker than normal fudge due to
the coconut oil. It's a fantastic sweet treat that the whole
family will love.

INGREDIENTS

Coconut oil

Two and a half cups of dairy free chocolate chips

Half a cup of coconut milk

A quarter of a cup of honey

An eighth of a teaspoon of salt

A teaspoon of vanilla extract

DIRECTIONS

Pour half a cup of coconut milk into the crockpot before adding in all of the rest of the ingredients, except for the vanilla extract. Cook it on high for two hours. Add the vanilla, stir it and then turn the crock pot off and leave it uncovered for three hours. Once it has cooled down, stir it well for about 10 minutes. Put it into a greased container and leave it to cool in the fridge overnight.

Pumpkin Pudding

This really tasty pudding is perfect to counteract those sweet cravings on a weekday and is really easy to make the night before, ready for a great family dinner. You can always swap out the pumpkin for apple or any other fruit if you prefer.

INGREDIENTS

Three tablespoons of melted coconut oil

Three cups of pureed pumpkin

Two cups of coconut milk

Three eggs

Half a cup of maple syrup

Two teaspoons of pumpkin pie spice

One and a half tablespoons of vanilla extract

Three tablespoons of coconut flour

A teaspoon of baking powder

DIRECTIONS

Mix all of the ingredients together and then put into the crock pot and cook on low for around seven hours until there is a crust on top but it remains a pudding consistency underneath.

Crock Pot Dough Balls

These make a great and quick dessert, perfect for after a heavy Sunday roast with the family, kids absolutely love them. If you have a large crockpot then you can increase a number of ingredients here, and the kids will love them.

INGREDIENTS

A third of a cup of coconut flour

Three eggs

Half a teaspoon of baking soda

Five tablespoons of coconut oil

Two tablespoons of honey

A cup of honey
Four tablespoons of coconut oil, melted
A tablespoon of cinnamon

DIRECTIONS

Mix all the dough ingredients together and split into dough balls. Then mix the honey, coconut oil and cinnamon together into a small bowl and dip each dough ball into it before placing all the dough balls into the crock pot. Cook on low for one and a half hours.

This chapter has provided a wide variety of recipe ideas to create wonderful paleo desserts easily in the crockpot. Whether you are looking for a fruit-based classic crumble or a non-dairy chocolate cake, I hope you found everything you were looking for here.

A paleo lifestyle can be challenging, particularly when it comes to avoiding processed sugars and dairy as cravings and temptations are there around every corner and you need really strong willpower to avoid giving in and buying that cream bun that is calling to you.

All of the desserts featured in this book use maple syrup and coconut sugar rather than any kind of refined sugars, helping you to beat those cravings and enjoy a natural sugar fix within the confines of a paleo diet.

The non-dairy fudge is a particular favorite of mine, and all of these dishes are slow cooked in the crock pot meaning you can create them overnight to have the next day or put them onto cook in the afternoon, ready for your evening meal that night.

Minimum fuss, minimum washing up, and completely healthy, all of these great dessert recipes are guaranteed to please all of the family and have them asking for more.

Chapter 14: More Quick And Easy Recipes

While most quick and easy recipes require the use of a crock pot, the following do not. They are still quick and easy and require a minimal number of ingredients. From stews, and seafood, to desserts and snacks, there is definitely something that will satisfy any craving that you may have! Just because you are switching to a healthier lifestyle by going to Paleo foods, does not mean that you should have to deprive yourself of those sweets and desserts. Enjoy!

Hunter's Stew

INGREDIENTS

2 pounds of beef, cubed

2 dozen blueberries

2 cups of baby carrots, sliced

Butter (to taste)

Coconut oil

 Salt and Pepper

Garlic powder

1 onion, sliced

DIRECTIONS

Cook the beef in coconut oil until it is browned. Add your seasoning until it is to your liking. Mix in your blueberries, carrots, and onion for the last 10 minutes of cooking. Your stew is ready when the carrots are tender.

Sweet Potato Pancakes

INGREDIENTS

1 sweet potato

Half an onion

2 eggs

1/2 tablespoon of coconut flour

1/2 teaspoon of salt and pepper

2 tablespoons of coconut oil

DIRECTIONS

Shred the sweet potato and the half of an onion. Squeeze the potato and onion in a cheesecloth to remove any excess moisture. Mix the eggs, coconut flour, salt, and pepper together in a medium-sized bowl. Add in the dried onion and sweet potato. In a pan or skillet, heat the coconut oil, and once it is hot add small amounts of the mixture to the pan. Cook until golden brown on both sides.

Egg Casserole Bites

INGREDIENTS

1 lb. ground beef

1 medium onion, diced

1 tbsp. extra virgin olive oil

1 1/2 dozen eggs

2 cups broccoli, chopped

1 cup cheddar cheese, shredded

DIRECTIONS

Over medium heat, saute the onion in olive oil for 2 to 3 minutes. Once, the onion is sautéed, add the ground beef to the skillet and cook until brown. Preheat oven to 350 degrees and grease the muffin tin. Beat the eggs well and add the broccoli, beef mixture, and cheese. Mix thoroughly. Using a measuring cup, scoop the mixture into the muffin cups and bake for 20 to 25 minutes until it is cooked through. Allow the bites to cool slightly before removing from the tin.

Shrimp Scampi

INGREDIENTS

2 lbs. large wild shrimp, peeled and deveined

4 Tbsp. grassfed butter

3 cloves minced garlic

2 lemons (organic)

3 zucchini (medium sized and cut into noodles)

DIRECTIONS

Lightly steam the noodles until they are almost tender. In a large skillet, on medium-high heat, heat 2 tbsp. of butter. Add the garlic into the butter and stir. Add shrimp, and sear for 1 to 2 minutes on each side. Add lemon juice, salt, and pepper to taste. Add in the zucchini noodles and toss in the sauce to mix the shrimp and noodles. Serve.

Quick Lunch Wraps Paleo

INGREDIENTS
3 eggs, large
2 tbsp. arrowroot powder
2 pinches of unprocessed salt
1 handful of parsley or salad greens
1 tsp. fresh herbs (Thyme, Tarragon, or Basil)

DIRECTIONS
Add ingredients to blender: arrowroot, eggs, salt, parsley or greens, herbs. Blend well, liquifying greens as much as possible. A small blender will work well. Brush an 8-inch pan with olive oil and heat the pan over medium-low heat. Pour ¼ cup of batter into the pan and swirl it around to make it circular. When it begins to get firm and can pull away from the pan, flip it over and cook briefly. Repeat with the remainder of the batter.

Use any kind of filling that you like. Chicken salad is always a good option.

Fish and Chips (Paleo)

INGREDIENTS
1 lb cod, wild caught
2 cups of coconut oil for frying
1 cup of almond flour
2 organic eggs
1/2 cup of coconut milk
1 tsp. of sea salt

DIRECTIONS
In a bowl, combine eggs, salt, coconut milk and almond flour. Mix well. Cut the cod into thin strips and place in the batter. Fry in coconut oil until golden brown.

SWEET POTATO CHIPS

INGREDIENTS
Sweet potatoes (5 medium sized)
Coconut Oil (3 cups)
Sea Salt (2 tsp.)
Pepper (to taste)

DIRECTIONS
Peel and thinly slice the sweet potatoes. Salt and pepper before placing them into a skillet or fryer. Fry in the coconut oil until they are brown. Remove and place on a paper towel to absorb the grease. Enjoy!

Sugar and Cinnamon Coconut Crisps

INGREDIENTS

2 tbsp. ghee or organic butter

4 cups of unsweetened, coarse coconut flakes

2 tsp. cinnamon

½ tsp of Stevia

½ tsp. of sea salt

DIRECTIONS

Melt the butter in a medium skillet over medium heat. Stir in the coconut flakes with a wooden spoon to coat with the melted butter until it turns a golden brown. Add in the salt, Stevia, and cinnamon and stir well. Remove from heat and place in a glass bowl. It turns crispy as it cools. Store at room temperature.

Chocolate Turtles

INGREDIENTS

¾ cup of melted dairy-free chocolate chips

6 dates, with pit, removed and cut in half

48 pecan halves, raw

DIRECTIONS
Cut dates lengthwise and remove the pit. Shape each piece into a circle with your fingers. Place pieces of parchment paper that are lining a baking sheet. Press pecan halves into the center of the date circles and arrange them to look like a flower. In a double broiler, melt chocolate chips. Spoon ½ tsp. of the melted chocolate onto the pecans. Flip your turtle over and press gently on it so that the chocolate reaches the parchment paper. Repeat for the remaining dates and set in freezer for 5 minutes to harden. Drop each hardened turtle into the melted chocolate until the back is covered. Place on baking sheet to cool.

Coconut Bars

INGREDIENTS

1 cup of unsweetened shredded coconut

1/4 cup agave or pure maple syrup

2 tbsp virgin coconut oil

1/2 tsp pure vanilla extract

1/8 tsp salt

DIRECTIONS

Combine all ingredients in a food processor. Compress into any small and refrigerate for an hour before trying to cut. (Or freeze for 15 minutes.) Can be stored in the fridge or freezer, for at least a few weeks.

Brownie Bites

INGREDIENTS

1 and ½ cup of walnuts

A pinch of salt

1 Cup pitted dates

1 tsp. vanilla

1/3 cup unsweetened cocoa powder

DIRECTIONS

In a blender or food processor, add walnuts and salt. Mix until finely ground. Add dates, cocoa powder, and vanilla to the blender. Blend well. While blending, add drops of water to make the mixture stick together. Transfer mixture into a bowl, and using your hands, form small round balls. Store in an airtight bag or container.

Coconut Cream and Grilled Peaches

INGREDIENTS

3 peaches, halved with pit removed

1 tsp. vanilla

¼ cup of chopped walnuts

1 Can of refrigerated coconut milk

Cinnamon (for taste)

DIRECTIONS

Place the peaches on the grill over medium-low heat, with the cut side down and cook until soft. Spoon cream from the top of the chilled can of coconut milk and whip together with vanilla, using a hand mixer. Drizzle mixture over the grilled peach and sprinkle the cinnamon and chopped walnuts over the top.

Chocolate Chip Pie

INGREDIENTS

3 Eggs

1 cup of coconut sugar

¼ cup of coconut flour

10 ounces of dairy free chocolate chips

1 cup grass fed butter, melted

DIRECTIONS

Preheat the oven to 325 degrees and grease a pie pan, preferably a 9-inch pan. In a separate bowl whip the eggs until they are foamy. Combine in coconut flour and sugar until well blended. Add in your butter while mixing well and stir in your dairy free chocolate chips. Pour into the greased pie pan and bake for 40 minutes. Remove from the oven and place foil over the top and cook for an additional 30 minutes. Serve warm.

Chapter 15: Slow Cooker Vegetarian Recipes

Now one of the biggest challenges with choosing a paleo lifestyle is trying to combine it with being a vegetarian. However, it's not impossible so if you are a paleo family, but one of your number rebels against the meat, or you have vegetarian friends to cater for, then these recipes should really help take the pain out of cooking for the veggies.

The good news they are also all made in the crock pot as well, so you won't be spending hours slaving over an alternative veggie meal either. It may mean investing in two crock pots, one for the meat dishes and one for the veggies but that's no bad thing.

It also means you can have one pot cooking breakfast while the other makes your dessert so why not go crock pot crazy!

Crock Pot Vegetable Lasagne

This delicious pasta dish works really well in the crockpot and has all of the traditional Italian flavors. If you need to cook for a vegetarian, you can't go wrong with this very classic dish.

INGREDIENTS

A 24-ounce jar of tomatoes
Nine sheets of lasagne pasta
Two and a half cups of vegetables of your choice
A teaspoon of chopped garlic
A tablespoon of olive oil
Fifteen ounces of ricotta cheese
One and a half cups of grated cheese

One egg

DIRECTIONS

Mix together one and a quarter cups of the grated cheese with the ricotta and the egg. Fry the vegetables with the garlic for a few minutes and add the tomato sauce to this pan. Remove the pan from the heat and spread a quarter of the mixture on the bottom of the crock pot. Layer lasagne sheets over it, then add a layer of the cheese mixture. Repeat the layers in this order. Once finished, sprinkle the rest of the grated cheese on top. Cook on a low heat for four hours or high heat for two hours.

Crock Pot Pepper and Kale Frittata with Feta Cheese

This frittata is really easy to make in the crock pot and a really tasty vegetarian crock pot option for friends. If you want to make it paleo just leave out the cheese or substitute with a non-dairy version.

INGREDIENTS

Five ounces of baby kale
Six ounces of diced and roasted red pepper
A quarter of a cup of onion, sliced
Four ounces of feta
Eight beaten eggs
Half a teaspoon of all purpose seasoning

DIRECTIONS

Wash the kale and saute in a pan for 3-4 minutes, then transfer into the crock pot. Add all of the rest of the ingredients into the crock pot and stir well to make sure they are all properly combined. Cook the mixture on low for 2-3 hours until the frittata is properly set and the cheese has all melted. This meal can be kept in the fridge for a few days and reheated in the microwave.

Crockpot Minestrone Soup

The other type of meal which a crockpot is great for creating is any kind of soup as the slow method of cooking really brings out all of the flavors. Why not try out this vegetarian minestrone soup as a starter for all the family and then experiment with the ingredients to create a wide variety of soup dishes in the crockpot for the whole family.

INGREDIENTS

A diced onion
Three crushed garlic cloves
Three peeled and chopped carrots
A tin of tomatoes
Two tins of cannellini beans
Three cups of vegetable stock
Three cups of water
Eight ounces of pasta
Twelve asparagus spears, chopped
A cup of peas

A six-ounce bag of spinach
A third of a cup of grated cheese

DIRECTIONS

Put the onions, beans, tomatoes, stock, water, garlic and carrots into the crockpot together and cook on low for four to six hours. Fifteen minutes before the time is up, add in the asparagus, spinach, peas and pasta and then continue to cook on low. Stir in the grated cheese just before serving.

Crock Pot Omelette

A classic dish, this vegetarian omelet can easily be adapted to make it paleo, but this option is just a traditional vegetarian version which can be slow cooked in the crock pot for added convenience.

INGREDIENTS

Six eggs
Half a cup of milk
A quarter of a teaspoon of salt
An eighth of a teaspoon of garlic powder
An eighth of a teaspoon of chili powder
A cup of broccoli
A sliced red pepper
A chopped onion
A crushed garlic clove
Grated cheese

DIRECTIONS

Take a bowl and mix together the milk, eggs, chili powder, garlic powder and salt and pepper. Put this mixture into the crockpot along with all of the rest of the ingredients apart from the cheese. Cook it on high heat for two hours. Once done, sprinkle over with the cheese and serve.

Curried Vegetables With Chickpea

This Indian inspired vegetable dish features a rainbow of intense flavors through the curry powder, cayenne pepper, and ginger and provides a really tasty and filling meal which will enhance any dinner party menu.

INGREDIENTS

A teaspoon of olive oil
One chopped onion
Two chopped sweet potatoes
A tablespoon of salt
A tablespoon of curry powder
A tablespoon of ginger
Three crushed garlic cloves
An eighth of a teaspoon of cayenne pepper
Two cups of vegetable stock
Two tins of chickpeas
Two chopped peppers
A head of cauliflower in florets
A tin of tomatoes
A quarter of a teaspoon of pepper

A bag of baby spinach
A cup of coconut milk

DIRECTIONS

Saute the onions and sweet potatoes in a pan together for about five minutes. Stir in the curry powder, garlic, ginger and cayenne pepper and cook for a further 30 seconds. Pour in a quarter of a cup of the stock. Put all of this mixture from the pan, into the crock pot. Add the remainder of the items, except for the spinach and coconut milk. Stir to mix well and cook on a high heat for four hours. When ready, stir in the spinach and coconut milk and cook for a few more minutes before serving.

Cauliflower Bolognese

This unusual slow cooked dish offers a complete alternative to pasta using courgettes instead of actual pasta, to create a full paleo version of the classic Bolognese sauce, and this one is also completely vegetarian. Dig out your spiralizer and enjoy!

INGREDIENTS

One head of cauliflower in florets
Three-quarters of a cup of onion
Two crushed garlic cloves
Two teaspoons of oregano
One teaspoon of basil
Two tins of tomatoes
Half a cup of vegetable stock
A quarter of a teaspoon of red pepper flakes
Five large courgettes

DIRECTIONS

Put all of the ingredients, apart from the courgettes, into the crockpot and stir together well. Cook on high for three and a half hours. Once cooked, use a masher to mash up the cauliflower to create the Bolognese texture. Use a spiralizer to create courgette noodles and spoon the Bolognese onto the noodles to serve.

Using the slow cooker to create traditional, unusual and tempting vegetarian meals is really easy, so there is no reason why you can't combine a paleo and a vegetarian diet together. Some of these recipes may contain cheese or other non-paleo elements, but they can all be easily adapted.

From a classic lasagne to a Bolognese using courgette instead of pasta, there are hundreds of vegetarian dishes to choose from, all of which provide nutritious and delicious meal options for all the family.

Paleo doesn't have to mean meat or fish all the time, it is perfectly possible to throw in the odd vegetarian dish into a paleo diet as long as you make sure to avoid the dairy which is often a common feature of vegetarian food.

Go for the tomato-based sauces and flavors rather than cream or cheese, and there won't be any difficulty combining the two, or if you really can't resist a cream or cheese-based dish then try some of the non-dairy alternatives to cream and cheese and treat yourself that way.

Vegetables are perfect for slow cooking and using the crock pot to break them down to create wonderful flavorsome soups is another way to be healthy and combine paleo with vegetarian.

Or if you want to include some meat then simply adapt the vegetarian soup recipe and replace the vegetable stock with chicken or beef stock to create the perfect meat-flavoured soup option.

Again, avoid the cream-based recipes if you want to stick to the healthy options, but there are plenty of tomato and stock-based soup choices out there, the possibilities are endless really. All you need to do is throw the vegetables of your choice into the liquid base and cook slowly for hours, and hey presto, your slow cooker will produce whatever flavor of soup takes your fancy. It might need a few minutes in the blender to really smooth out the soup consistency, but that's easy enough to do. Just don't be tempted to add a bread roll to it!

Conclusion

So what do you think? Each one of those 30 recipes required no more than five ingredients and about as many minutes of preparation before you leave the house in the morning. We also added in a variety of other quick and tasty recipes that are sure to satisfy any craving or urge you may have. Making it even easier to stick with your healthy eating on the Paleo diet. It is amazing how that little effort can result in coming home from a long day to an already prepared, home cooked meal. More importantly, each one of these meals follows the paleo eating protocol so you can take advantage of all the health benefits of adding nutrient dense, inflammation reducing foods to your diet while avoiding the disease inducing, a fat stimulating diet that is so prevalent in America today.

What are you waiting for? Join the millions of people that have joined the paleo movement for a real and noticeable change in their health and wellbeing. Never before has it been so easy to make the change. With the time you have spent reading through the recipes included in this book, you could have prepped and set your slow cooker with a delicious and nutritious meal for you and your friends or family. Take the challenge and try some out. Post on your social media accounts all the masterpieces that you have created and wow your friends! These recipes are even suitable for your whole family, to get everyone on a healthier lifestyle. They will surely be envious of the delectable culinary creations, and shocked by the physical transformation that you go through as you adopt the paleo lifestyle!

Closing

Will you leave me a review?

I really want to thank you for reading this book. I sincerely hope that you enjoyed it. I would love your feedback to improve my writing on this piece and future stories. If you got value out of this work, would you mind leaving me a review on Amazon? Your feedback is very important to my development as an author.

Recipe Index

Almond Butter

-Chocolate Almond Butter Oatmeal 35

Apples

-Roasted Pork and Apples 18

-BBQ Chicken Apple Stew 33

-Crock Pot Apple Breakfast Butter 53

-Crock Pot Apples and Cabbage 83

-Apple Puree 93

-Crock Pot Apple Pie Sauce 96

-Quinoa and Apple Crock Pot 94

Avocado

-Avocado Egg Bowls 55

Bacon

-Hawaiian Pork 27

-Sweet Potato and Egg Skillet 54

Beef

-Slow Cooker Pull-Apart Beef 16

-Coconut Curry Beef 25

-Red Wine Beef Roast 28

-Irish Beef Stew 30

-Pepper Encrusted Pot Roast 34

-Thai Beef 38

-BBQ Beef Ribs 42

-Beef Cabbage Stew 43

-Beef Chili 47

-Hunter's Stew 105

-Beef and Kale Salad 76

-Meatballs and Greens 77

-Crock Pot Ribs with Ginger 71

-Crock Pot Beef with Kale 71

-Crock Pot Paleo Stew 81

Brownie

-Brownie Bites 112

Cabbage

-Pork and Cabbage Stew 28

-Beef Cabbage Stew 43

-Crock Pot Apples and Cabbage 83

Capers

-Rosemary Capered Eggs 56

Chicken

--Healthy Pad Thai 14

-Chicken Vegetable Broth 26

-Maple Syrup Chicken 20

-Salsa Verde Chicken 21

-Chicken Satay 22

-Whole Chicken in a Pot 23

-Southwest Chicken 29

-BBQ Chicken Apple Stew 33

-Butternut Squash Chicken Soup 36

-Pumpkin Chicken Stew 41

-Arroz Con Pollo 44

-Meatballs and Greens 77

-Vegetable Noodles with Cream Sauce 78

-Chicken Lettuce Taco Wraps 80

-Lettuce Crock Pot Tacos 70

-Crock Pot Chili Chicken 72

-Crock Pot Roast Chicken Dinner 73

-Crock Pot Paleo Chicken 74

-Crock Pot Roast-Mississippi Style 86

-Crock Pot Chicken Salsa 89

Chocolate

-Chocolate Almond Butter Oatmeal 35

-Chocolate Turtles 111

-Brownie Bites 112

-Chocolate Chip Pie 114

-Non-Chocolate Paleo Cookies 96

-Non-Dairy Chocolate Cake 98

-Fudge without Dairy 100

Coconut

-Healthy Pad Thai 14

-Coconut Curry Beef 25

-Thai Beef 38

-Sugar and Cinnamon Coconut Crisps 110

-Coconut Bars 111

-Coconut Cream and Grilled Peaches 113

-Sweet Vanilla and Chia Treat 57

-Meatballs and Greens 77

Eggs

-Egg Casserole Bites 107

-Sweet Potato and Egg Skillet 54

-Avocado Egg Bowls 55

-Sardine Egg Explosion 55

-Rosemary Capered Eggs 56

-Summer Squash Breakfast 57

-Crock Pot Omelette 58

-Crock Pot Frittata 59

-Crock Pot Breakfast Pie 64

-Crock Pot Breakfast Casserole 65

-Crock Pot Paleo Mexican Breakfast 65

-Crock Pot Sausage and Egg Breakfast 66

-Crock Pot Dough Balls 102

Fish

-Fish and Chips 109

-Sardine Egg Explosion 55

-Creamy Cod with Pesto 79

Oatmeal

-Pumpkin Pie Oatmeal 19

-Chocolate Almond Butter Oatmeal 35

-Crock Pot Oatmeal with Squash 58

Pancakes

-Sweet Potato Pancakes 106

Pasta

-Shrimp Scampi 108

-Vegetable Noodles with Cream Sauce 78

-Crock Pot Vegetable Lasagna 115

Peaches

-Coconut Cream and Grilled Peaches 113

Pie

-Pumpkin Pie Oatmeal 19

-Chocolate Chip Pie 114

-Crock Pot Pear Crumble 99

Pork

-Roasted Pork and Apples 18

-Hawaiian Pork 27

-Pork and Cabbage 28

-Sausage and Kale Soup 32

-Sausage and Peppers 39

-BBQ Pork Ribs 46

-Sweet Potato and Egg Skillet 54

-Crock Pot Pulled Pork Breakfast 62

-Crock Pot Sausage and Egg Breakfast 66

-Crock Pot Pork Ramen 87

Pumpkin

-Pumpkin Pie Oatmeal 19

-Pumpkin Chicken Stew 41

-Paleo Spicy Soup 84

-Pumpkin Puree 95

-Pumpkin Pudding 101

Sardine

-Sardine Egg Explosion 55

Sausage

-Sausage and Kale Soup 32

-Sausage and Peppers 39

Shrimp

-Shrimp Scampi 108

Smoothie

-Blackberry Pineapple Smoothie 58

Soups

-Chicken Vegetable Broth 26

-Sausage and Kale Soup 32

-Butternut Squash Chicken Soup 36

-Creamy Butternut Squash Soup 39

-Beef Chili 47

-Delectable Broccoli Soup 75

-Crock Pot Minestrone Soup 117

-Paleo Spicy Soup 84

Squash

-Butternut Squash Chicken Soup 36

-Creamy Butternut Squash Soup 39

-Butternut Squash Vegetable Stew 45

-Summer Squash Breakfast 57

-Crock Pot Oatmeal with Squash 58

-Crock Pot Squash with Rosemary 90

Stews

-Pork and Cabbage Stew 28

-Irish Beef Stew 30

-BBQ Chicken Apple Stew 33

-Pumpkin Chicken Stew 41

-Beef Cabbage Stew 43

-Butternut Squash Vegetable Stew 45

-Beef Chili 47

-Hunter's Stew 39

-Crock Pot Paleo Stew 81

Made in the USA
Middletown, DE
10 June 2017